Presentable
Writing Clear Opinions

Robert Hickling | Jun Yashima

Australia · Brazil · Mexico · Singapore · United Kingdom · United States

Presentable—Writing Clear Opinions

Robert Hickling / Jun Yashima

© 2024 Cengage Learning K.K.

Photo Credits:
Cover: © Dreamstime.com; 11: © stock adobe.com; 19: © stock adobe.com; 27: © stock adobe.com; 35: © stock adobe.com; 43: © stock adobe.com; 51: © NASA Image Library; 59: © stock adobe.com; 67: © stock adobe.com; 75: © stock adobe.com; 83: © stock adobe.com; 91: © stock adobe.com; 99: © stock adobe.com; 107: © stock adobe.com; 115: © stock adobe.com; 123: © stock adobe.com;

For permission to use material from this textbook or product, e-mail to **eltjapan@cengage.com**

ISBN: 978-4-86312-425-7

National Geographic Learning | Cengage Learning K.K.
No. 2 Funato Building 5th Floor
1-11-11 Kudankita, Chiyoda-ku
Tokyo 102-0073
Japan

Tel: 03-3511-4392
Fax: 03-3511-4391

はしがき

　本書は、英語を用いて情報、意見、考えを的確に伝えられるようになることを目的としたテキストです。最近では、ソーシャルメディアやオンライン会議ツールなどの普及により、日本にいても英語によるコミュニケーションの機会を作ることが以前よりもはるかに容易になりました。しかし、それにもかかわらず、プレゼンテーションやディスカッションになると、英語を使って情報や意見を的確に発信できる人は決して多くありません。これには語彙力や表現力、トピックに関する知識の不足など、複合的な要因が絡んでいると考えられます。

　本書は、様々なトピックを題材に、語彙や表現パターン、背景知識を身につけながら、学習者が無理なく自然な形で英語の発信力を向上させられるように構成されています。各 Unit には一つのテーマが与えられており、テーマに関する簡単な質問に答える **Get Started** から始まります。**Get Started** で問題意識を高めたら、**Read About It** でプレゼンテーションやエッセイの典型的な構成パターンに従って書かれたパッセージを読み、**Get It Right** でその理解を確認し、**Paragraph Summary** でパラグラフ構成を学びます。続いて、**Vocabulary Builder** で重要語句を深掘りし、それらの語句を能動的に使えるようにするための練習をします。**Brainstorming** では Unit のテーマに関連するトピックについてブレインストーミングを行い、自分の考えを発信するための準備をします。さらに、**Say It Clearly** でプレゼンテーションを効果的に行うための表現方法を学び、**Now You Try** で実際に学んだ表現を運用する練習をします。最後の **Present Your Ideas** で、Unit を通して学んだことをふまえて、与えられたトピックに関するプレゼンテーションの原稿を作成します。

　各 Unit のテーマは、「オンライン授業と対面授業」「ストレスの原因と影響」「ホームステイの長所と短所」のような大学生に馴染みのあるものから「AI 利用の是非」「地方過疎化の問題点と解決策」「プラスチックごみ問題」のような社会問題まで多岐にわたっています。様々な話題やプレゼンテーションのパターンに触れることで、日常的なコミュニケーションだけでなく、ディスカッションやディベートのようなアカデミックな場面での発信力も向上させられるようにバランスよく構成されています。

　このテキストを通じて、みなさんが自信を持って英語で情報や意見を交換できるようになることを願っております。

著者一同

Table of Contents

		Title
Unit	1	**Online Learning vs. Traditional Learning**
Unit	2	**Living Alone or Living with a Roommate**
Unit	3	**Exploring Academic Environments & Lifestyles**
Unit	4	**Is Honesty Always the Best Policy?**
Unit	5	**Examining Gap Years**
Unit	6	**Is Space Exploration Worth the Cost?**
Unit	7	**Leisure Activities & Vacations**
Unit	8	**The Dynamics of Friendships**
Unit	9	**Stress Among University Students**
Unit	10	**The Baby Bust in Japan**
Unit	11	**The Upsides & Downsides of Social Media**
Unit	12	**Homestay or Stay Home?**
Unit	13	**AI: A Double-Edged Sword**
Unit	14	**The Rural Depopulation Challenge**
Unit	15	**Plastic Waste Issues & Actions**

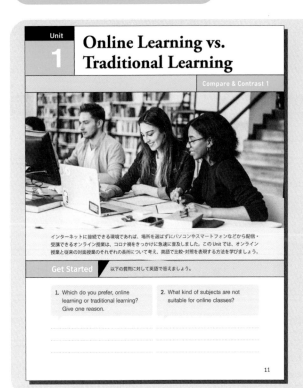

Unit は 8 ページ構成です。以下に、それぞれの項目や設問の目的と使い方を説明します。

Get Started

各 Unit で扱われているテーマに関して、英語の質問に答えます。テーマに関する問題意識を高めるだけでなく、自分の考えを英語で表現するウォームアップを行います。

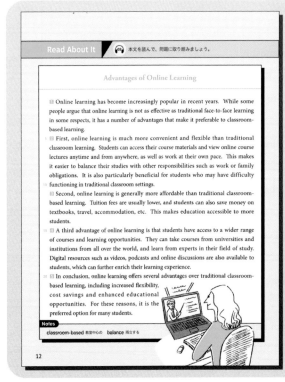

Read About It

それぞれの Unit のテーマに関して、プレゼンテーションやエッセイの典型的なパターンで書かれた 250 語ほどの英文を読みます。

Get It Right

本文の内容に合うように、( ) の中から適切な語句を選びましょう。

1. Online course lectures are (a. more easily accessible b. generally shorter) than face-to-face lectures.

2. (a. Classroom-based learning is more affordable than online learning. b. Online learning is more cost effective than classroom-based learning.)

3. Online learning allows students to (a. take tests in the language of their choice b. take classes from multiple educational institutions).

Paragraph Summary

本文の語句を使い、各パラグラフを要約しましょう。
完成したら、音声を聞いて確認しましょう。

⬚ There are several advantages that make online learning preferable to
1. _____ classroom learning.

⬚ Online learning offers convenience and flexibility, allowing students to
2. _____ course materials and view lectures at any time and from any location.

⬚ Online learning is more 3. _____ than traditional learning, so students can save money on course books, travel, accommodation and so on.

⬚ Online learning offers a broader 4. _____ of courses and opportunities, connecting students globally and providing access to expert knowledge and digital
5. _____.

⬚ For these reasons — increased flexibility, cost savings and enhanced educational opportunities — online learning is the 6. _____ option for many students.

13

Get It Right

Read About It で読んだ英文の内容が理解できているか確認をします。2択の問題ですが、正しく理解していないと3問すべてに正解することは容易ではありません。全問正解を目指しましょう。

Paragraph Summary

Read About It の語句を使い、穴埋めをして要約文を完成させます。**Read About It** と同じパラグラフ構成になっていますので、パラグラフの構成を考えながら要約文を完成させましょう。

Vocabulary Builder

次の問題に取り組み、本 Unit に関連する重要語句の意味と使い方をマスターしましょう。

A 以下の語句の定義を下の a ～ h から選んで ____ に記入しましょう。

face-to-face	____	a at a speed suitable for the person
feedback	____	b in-person
remotely	____	c to communicate, work or participate in an activity together
flexible	____	d separated or not connected
transportation	____	e able to be modified easily
at one's own pace	____	f from a distance
isolated	____	g the movement of people or goods from one place to another
interact	____	h information given to someone about their performance or work

B A で学んだ語句を使い、以下の英文を完成させましょう。

1. The professor taught all her classes _____ last year.

2. Working from home allows me to have a more _____ schedule and a better work-life balance.

3. The manager emphasized the importance of _____ communication in the workplace.

4. The teacher provided valuable _____ on my presentation.

5. Painting allows for creative expression _____.

6. Some remote workers feel _____ from their coworkers.

7. Electric cars are becoming more and more popular as a means of _____.

8. It's a good idea to _____ with your classmates to build a supportive learning community.

14

Vocabulary Builder

各 Unit のテーマに関係する重要語句の意味を A で確認し、 B でその語句を使った例文を完成させることで、語句の使い方を学習します。

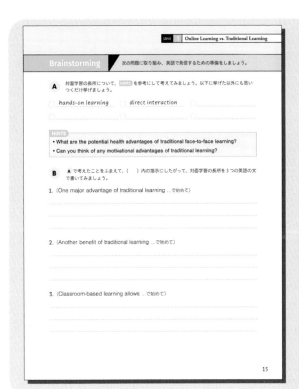

Brainstorming　次の問題に取り組み、英語で発信するための準備をしましょう。

A　対面学習の長所について、HINTS を参考にして考えてみましょう。以下に挙げた以外にも思いつくだけ挙げましょう。

☐ *hands-on learning*　　☐ *direct interaction*　　☐

☐　　　　　　　　　　　　☐　　　　　　　　　　　　☐

HINTS
- What are the potential health advantages of traditional face-to-face learning?
- Can you think of any motivational advantages of traditional learning?

B　A で考えたことをふまえて、（　）内の指示にしたがって、対面学習の長所を 3 つの英語の文で書いてみましょう。

1. (One major advantage of traditional learning ...で始めて)

2. (Another benefit of traditional learning ...で始めて)

3. (Classroom-based learning allows ...で始めて)

15

Brainstorming

各 Unit のテーマに関係するトピックについて、まずどのようなことが考えられるかブレインストーミングをします。続いて、そのことを英語で表現するための準備練習を行います。

Say It Clearly

イントロダクションを効果的に行う

口頭プレゼンテーションがエッセイライティングと大きく異なる点は、聴衆とのコミュニケーションを伴うことです。聴衆の関心を引き、的確にメッセージを伝えるプレゼンテーションを行うには、イントロダクションを次の順序で構成すると効果的です。※ Purpose は省略されることもあります。

Welcoming → Topic → Purpose → Preview

Useful Expressions

WELCOMING（聴衆へ挨拶する）
- **Good [morning/afternoon]**, everyone.
- **Hello** everyone.

TOPIC（プレゼンテーションのトピックを伝える）
- The **[topic/subject] of my presentation** is the benefits of AI in education.
- **What I am going to talk about** today is the pros and cons of remote work.
- Today **I am here to talk to you about** the effects of air pollution on the environment.

PURPOSE（プレゼンテーションの目的・ねらいを伝える）
- The **[purpose/objective/aim] of this presentation** is to show how to make the most of college life.
- **My objective** today is to raise awareness of the risks associated with smoking.

PREVIEW（プレゼンテーションの進め方を予告する）
- My [presentation/talk] is **divided into two parts**.
- I'm going to **tell you three reasons why** learning English is beneficial.

16

Say It Clearly

英語でプレゼンテーションを行ったり、エッセイを書いたりする際に、効果的な英語表現を学習します。

Now You Try

以下の 4 つの英文を最も自然な流れになるように並び替えて、口頭プレゼンテーションのイントロダクションを完成させましょう。

A. The purpose of this presentation is to offer practical advice for a healthy lifestyle.

B. Good morning, everyone.

C. I will give you three key tips that you can incorporate into your daily life to improve your overall health and well-being.

D. Today I'm excited to talk to you on the topic of health.

上で学んだことを参考にして、「対面学習の長所」というテーマのプレゼンテーションのイントロダクションを書いてみましょう。

17

Now You Try

Say It Clearly で学習した英語表現を実際に運用する練習をします。実際に運用することで、学習した表現が自分のものになっていきます。

Present Your Ideas

この Unit で学習したことをもとに、対面学習の長所についてのプレゼンテーション原稿を完成させましょう。

1 Hello everyone. Today, I'm going to talk about

2 One major advantage of traditional learning

3 Another benefit

4 We should also consider

5 In conclusion,

18

Present Your Ideas

各 Unit で学習したことをふまえて、与えられたトピックについて、プレゼンテーションの原稿を自分で作成してみます。まずは書いてみて、次に学習したことを振り返り修正しながら、よりわかりやすい文章にしていきましょう。

音声ファイルの利用方法

 のアイコンがある箇所の音声ファイルにアクセスできます。

https://ngljapan.com/prstbl-audio/

❶ 上記の URL にアクセス、または QR コードをスマートフォンなどのリーダーでスキャン

❷ 表示されるファイル名をクリックして音声ファイルをダウンロードまたは再生

Online Learning vs. Traditional Learning

インターネットに接続できる環境であれば、場所を選ばずにパソコンやスマートフォンなどから配信・受講できるオンライン授業は、コロナ禍をきっかけに急速に普及しました。この Unit では、オンライン授業と従来の対面授業のそれぞれの長所について考え、英語で比較・対照を表現する方法を学びましょう。

Get Started

以下の質問に対して英語で答えましょう。

1. Which do you prefer, online learning or traditional learning? Give one reason.

2. What kind of subjects are not suitable for online classes?

Advantages of Online Learning

1 Online learning has become increasingly popular in recent years. While some people argue that online learning is not as effective as traditional face-to-face learning in some respects, it has a number of advantages that make it preferable to classroom-based learning.

5 **2** First, online learning is much more convenient and flexible than traditional classroom learning. Students can access their course materials and view online course lectures anytime and from anywhere, as well as work at their own pace. This makes it easier to balance their studies with other responsibilities such as work or family obligations. It is also particularly beneficial for students who may have difficulty

10 functioning in traditional classroom settings.

3 Second, online learning is generally more affordable than traditional classroom-based learning. Tuition fees are usually lower, and students can also save money on textbooks, travel, accommodation, etc. This makes education accessible to more students.

15 **4** A third advantage of online learning is that students have access to a wider range of courses and learning opportunities. They can take courses from universities and institutions from all over the world, and learn from experts in their field of study. Digital resources such as videos, podcasts and online discussions are also available to students, which can further enrich their learning experience.

20 **5** In conclusion, online learning offers several advantages over traditional classroom-based learning, including increased flexibility, cost savings and enhanced educational opportunities. For these reasons, it is the preferred option for many students.

Notes

classroom-based 教室中心の　balance 両立する

12

Get It Right

本文の内容に合うように、（　）の中から適切な語句を選びましょう。

1. Online course lectures are (a. more easily accessible b. generally shorter) than face-to-face lectures.

2. (a. Classroom-based learning is more affordable than online learning. b. Online learning is more cost effective than classroom-based learning.)

3. Online learning allows students to (a. take tests in the language of their choice b. take classes from multiple educational institutions).

Paragraph Summary

 本文の語句を使い、各パラグラフを要約しましょう。
完成したら、音声を聞いて確認しましょう。

1 There are several advantages that make online learning preferable to 1............................ classroom learning.

2 Online learning offers convenience and flexibility, allowing students to 2............................ course materials and view lectures at any time and from any location.

3 Online learning is more 3............................ than traditional learning, so students can save money on course books, travel, accommodation and so on.

4 Online learning offers a broader 4............................ of courses and opportunities, connecting students globally and providing access to expert knowledge and digital 5............................ .

5 For these reasons — increased flexibility, cost savings and enhanced educational opportunities — online learning is the 6............................ option for many students.

13

A 以下の語句の定義を下の a 〜 h から選んで .... に記入しましょう。

face-to-face	....	a	at a speed suitable for the person
feedback	....	b	in-person
remotely	....	c	to communicate, work or participate in an activity together
flexible	....	d	separated or not connected
transportation	....	e	able to be modified easily
at one's own pace	....	f	from a distance
isolated	....	g	the movement of people or goods from one place to another
interact	....	h	information given to someone about their performance or work

B **A** で学んだ語句を使い、以下の英文を完成させましょう。

1. The professor taught all her classes .... last year.

2. Working from home allows me to have a more .... schedule and a better work-life balance.

3. The manager emphasized the importance of .... communication in the workplace.

4. The teacher provided valuable .... on my presentation.

5. Painting allows for creative expression ....

6. Some remote workers feel .... from their coworkers.

7. Electric cars are becoming more and more popular as a means of ....

8. It's a good idea to .... with your classmates to build a supportive learning community.

Brainstorming

次の問題に取り組み、英語で発信するための準備をしましょう。

A 対面学習の長所について、 HINTS を参考にして考えてみましょう。以下に挙げた以外にも思いつくだけ挙げましょう。

☐ *hands-on learning*　　☐ *direct interaction*　　☐ ....

☐ ....　　☐ ....　　☐ ....

HINTS

- What are the potential health advantages of traditional face-to-face learning?
- Can you think of any motivational advantages of traditional learning?

B **A** で考えたことをふまえて、（　　）内の指示にしたがって、対面学習の長所を 3 つの英語の文で書いてみましょう。

1. (One major advantage of traditional learning ...で始めて)

....

....

....

2. (Another benefit of traditional learning ...で始めて)

....

....

....

3. (Classroom-based learning allows ...で始めて)

....

....

....

イントロダクションを効果的に行う

口頭プレゼンテーションがエッセイライティングと大きく異なる点は、聴衆とのコミュニケーションを伴うことです。聴衆の関心を引き、的確にメッセージを伝えるプレゼンテーションを行うには、イントロダクションを次の順序で構成すると効果的です。※ Purpose は省略されることもあります。

Welcoming → Topic → Purpose → Preview

Useful Expressions

WELCOMING（聴衆へ挨拶する）

- **Good** {**morning/afternoon**}, everyone.
- **Hello** everyone.

TOPIC（プレゼンテーションのトピックを伝える）

- **The** {**topic/subject**} **of my presentation** is the benefits of AI in education.
- **What I am going to talk about** today is the pros and cons of remote work.
- Today **I am here to talk to you about** the effects of air pollution on the environment.

PURPOSE（プレゼンテーションの目的・ねらいを伝える）

- **The** {**purpose/objective/aim**} **of this presentation** is to show how to make the most of college life.
- **My objective** today is to raise awareness of the risks associated with smoking.

PREVIEW（プレゼンテーションの進め方を予告する）

- My {presentation/talk} is **divided into two parts**.
- I'm going to **tell you three reasons why** learning English is beneficial.

Now You Try

以下の４つの英文を最も自然な流れになるように並び替えて、口頭プレゼンテーションのイントロダクションを完成させましょう。

A. The purpose of this presentation is to offer practical advice for a healthy lifestyle.

B. Good morning, everyone.

C. I will give you three key tips that you can incorporate into your daily life to improve your overall health and well-being.

D. Today I'm excited to talk to you on the topic of health.

上で学んだことを参考にして、「対面学習の長所」というテーマのプレゼンテーションのイントロダクションを書いてみましょう。

....

....

....

....

....

....

....

....

Present Your Ideas

このUnitで学習したことをもとに、対面学習の長所についてのプレゼンテーション原稿を完成させましょう。

1 Hello everyone. Today, I'm going to talk about

....

....

....

2 One major advantage of traditional learning

....

....

....

3 Another benefit

....

....

....

4 We should also consider

....

....

....

5 In conclusion,

....

....

....

Living Alone or Living with a Roommate

大学進学、留学、就職などをきっかけに、親元を離れて新たな生活を始める人は多くいます。新生活を始める上で、一人暮らしをするか、ルームメイトと共同生活をするかは重要な選択の一つとなります。この Unit では、それぞれの長所について考え、英語で比較・対照を表現する方法を学びましょう。

Get Started

以下の質問に対して英語で答えましょう。

1. What are a few things to consider when deciding whether to live alone or with a roommate?

2. What type of person would be your ideal roommate?

The Benefits of Living Alone

 Living alone can be a very rewarding and liberating experience, especially for young people living away from home for the first time. While it may sound overwhelming to people who have never experienced living independently, it is worthy of consideration for a number of reasons.

5 ❷ One of the main benefits of living alone is independence. You have total control over your living space. You can arrange and decorate it to your liking and do household chores at your convenience. You can come and go as you please.

❸ Another big advantage of living by yourself is the privacy it offers. You don't have to share a bathroom, living room or any other common areas with anyone. You needn't
10 worry about making noise or bothering others. And you have the option of complete solitude whenever you need it.

❹ A third benefit of solo living is that it allows you to be more flexible with your schedule and routines. You can do things at your own pace, make decisions without consulting with others and change your plans at a moment's notice. The ability to be
15 flexible and adaptable helps reduce stress and makes daily life more enjoyable and satisfying.

❺ Finally, living alone fosters personal growth and development. It's a wonderful opportunity to learn more about yourself
20 and to discover talents that you never knew you had. Independent living also allows you to pursue your hobbies and interests and to concentrate on your goals without any outside distractions.

Notes

liberating 解放感のある　　overwhelming 圧倒的な、非常に大変な　　adaptable 適応できる、調整できる

Get It Right

本文の内容に合うように、（　　）の中から適切な語句を選びましょう。

1. Not having to concern yourself with disturbing others is an example of the
   (a. independence b. privacy) aspect of living alone.

2. Living alone provides you with the opportunity to (a. make new friends more
   easily b. have greater flexibility in managing your time).

3. Living alone (a. promotes self-discovery b. improves your interpersonal skills).

Paragraph Summary

本文の語句を使い、各パラグラフを要約しましょう。
完成したら音声を聞いて確認しましょう。

1 Although it may sound 1................................ to some, living alone can be beneficial
to people in different ways.

2 Living by yourself provides 2................................ by allowing you to have full control
over your living space, and to go out and return home whenever you like.

3 Living alone gives you 3............................. You don't have to share common areas
or worry about making noise, and you can enjoy complete 4........................... at any
time.

4 Solo living allows you to be more 5........................... with your schedule, decision-
making, etc. This lowers 6........................... and makes life more enjoyable and
fulfilling.

5 Living independently is an 7........................... for you to grow and develop as a
person. Moreover, it is a chance to spend more time on hobbies and pursue goals
without 8.....................

21

A 以下の語句の定義を下の a ～ h から選んで .... に記入しましょう。

solitude ....

distraction ....

chores ....

arrange ....

utilities ....

conflict ....

companionship ....

compromise ....

a essential services such as electricity, water and gas

b find common ground or a mutually acceptable agreement

c a clash or disagreement

d something that prevents you from concentrating

e organize or plan the details of something

f the state of being alone

g the enjoyment of spending time with other people

h routine tasks that need to be done around the house

B A で学んだ語句を使い、以下の英文を完成させましょう。

1. Every Sunday morning, I tackle a list of ...., including doing the laundry and vacuuming the carpet.

2. Paying the monthly .... is an essential responsibility for every homeowner.

3. Spending time in .... allows one to reflect on their actions.

4. Successful negotiations require a willingness to ....

5. The event planner will .... all the necessary details, such as food and decorations, to ensure a successful celebration.

6. Volunteers provide .... to elderly residents in nursing homes.

7. The noise from construction outside was a constant ...., making it difficult to concentrate on my work.

8. The .... between the two colleagues resulted in a tense working environment.

Brainstorming

次の問題に取り組み、英語で発信するための準備をしましょう。

A ルームシェアの長所について、**HINTS** を参考にして考えてみましょう。以下に挙げたもの以外にも思いつくだけ挙げましょう。

☐ security and safety ☐ help with chores ☐ ....

☐ .... ☐ .... ☐ ....

HINTS
- What are some financial advantages of living with a roommate?
- Are there any emotional benefits of having a roommate?

B **A** で考えたことをふまえて、（　　）内の指示にしたがって、ルームシェアの長所を3つの英語の文で書いてみましょう。

1. (Having a roommate ...で始めて)

....
....
....

2. (When you live with a roommate, ...で始めて)

....
....
....

3. (You and your roommate can ...で始めて)

....
....
....

２つの物事を対照して論じる

　２つの物事の特徴を引き比べて説明する場合や２つの異なる考えを対照して論じる場合には、両者の共通点や相違点を明確にする必要があります。２つの物事や考えに類似性があること、あるいは両者が対照的であることを示すには、以下のような表現が役に立ちます。

Useful Expressions

類似を表す前置詞

- Just **like** George, Emily is good at playing the piano.

類似を表す副詞

- Food prices have recently increased significantly. **Similarly**, oil prices have also seen a notable rise.

類似を表す接続詞

- **Just as** humans experience emotions, animals exhibit various feelings.

対照を表す前置詞

- **Unlike** his classmates, George enjoys studying statistics.

対照を表す副詞句

- His first book is a romantic comedy. **In contrast**, his second book is a crime thriller.
- Emma loves cats. **On the other hand**, her brother prefers dogs.

対照を表す接続詞

- Some children love to play outside, {**while/whereas**} others prefer staying indoors.

Now You Try

次の英文を読み、下の設問に答えましょう。

Christmas is a festive time of year in both the United States and Japan, but (❶). In the United States, many people attend church services on Christmas Eve and have family gatherings on Christmas Day. (❷), Christmas in Japan is generally viewed as a secular event with an emphasis on gift-giving and dining out, especially among young couples. ❸While Christmas in the United States is a time for family gatherings, for many in Japan it is primarily a romantic day.

Notes festive お祭り気分の、にぎやかな　secular 非宗教的な

1. 空欄❶に入る最も適切な文を以下から選びましょう。

　　a. the two countries have several things in common
　　b. there are some differences in the way it is celebrated
　　c. it is no longer regarded as a religious holiday
　　d. the history of Christmas is full of mystery

2. 空欄❷に入る最も適切な語句を以下から選びましょう。

　　a. In addition　　b. For example　　c. Unlike　　d. In contrast

3. 下線部❸を接続詞 but を用いた文に書き換えてみましょう。

....

....

....

Present Your Ideas

この Unit で学習したことをもとに、ルームシェアの長所についてのプレゼンテーション原稿を完成させましょう。

1 *Good afternoon. As you know, there are various types of living arrangements, each with its own unique features and advantages. Today, I'm here to discuss*

2 *First of all,*

3 *Second,*

4 *Third,*

5 *Finally,*

Exploring Academic Environments & Lifestyles

大学生活は、自身の興味や関心に基づいて専門的な学びを深めつつ、人間としての自己成長や将来の進路への準備の機会を与えてくれる貴重な時間です。当然ながら、高校までとは学びの内容も経験することも大きく異なります。この Unit では、大学と高校での学びの違いについて考えてみましょう。

Get Started

以下の質問に対して英語で答えましょう。

1. What are some things you miss about your high school days?

2. What was the biggest adjustment you had to make from high school to university?

....

....

....

....

....

....

Sizing Up Universities

1 Whether one chooses to attend a large university or a small university is often a matter of personal preference. Not surprisingly, small universities have fewer students, smaller campuses and fewer degree programs than large universities. However, there are a number of other differences that set small universities and large universities apart from each other.

2 Because classes are generally smaller, students attending small universities can receive more personalized attention from professors than they can at large universities. This allows for more interactive class discussions, and provides students with more opportunities to build stronger relationships with their peers. Additionally, small universities typically offer more hands-on learning experiences than large universities.

3 While small universities may offer a more limited choice of courses and programs than large universities, this can be advantageous for students. Smaller institutions have more flexibility in designing their curricula, as opposed to following standardized programs. This allows them to tailor their programs to the particular needs and interests of students.

4 Large universities attract students with a greater diversity of academic and cultural backgrounds than small institutions. This often results in more enriching class discussions and exposure to different perspectives. Big universities also tend to have more resources, including extensive library collections and services, state-of-the-art research facilities and greater employment assistance.

5 Another difference is the larger and more active alumni network that big universities have compared to smaller universities. As a result, students are more likely to make valuable connections for internships, jobs and other opportunities in the future.

Notes

degree 学位　state-of-the-art 最先端の

Get It Right

本文の内容に合うように、（　　）の中から適切な語句を選びましょう。

1. (a. Small universities   b. Large universities) offer more practical or experience-driven learning opportunities.

2. Small universities are more likely to follow (a. customized courses   b. standardized curricula) than large universities.

3. Compared to large universities, small universities have a (a. more   b. less) active alumni network.

Paragraph Summary

 本文の語句を使い、各パラグラフを要約しましょう。
完成したら音声を聞いて確認しましょう。

1️⃣ Attending a small or large university is often based on 1................................ choice. Besides enrollment, campus size and degree programs, they differ in several other ways.

2️⃣ Small universities provide 2................................ attention from professors, leading to more 3................................ discussions, stronger peer relationships and more hands-on learning.

3️⃣ Smaller institutions have greater 4................................ in curriculum design and can 5................................ their programs to the specific interests and needs of students.

4️⃣ Large universities attract a greater 6................................ of students than small universities, enriching class discussions and offering a wider range of viewpoints. They also provide more resources and employment assistance.

5️⃣ The larger 7................................ network of big universities increases the possibility for students to make important 8................................ for internships, jobs and other opportunities.

29

A 以下の語句の定義を下の a ～ h から選んで .... に記入しましょう。

distinct ....

resources ....

tailor ....

diversity ....

specialized ....

supervise ....

responsibility ....

alumni ....

a designed for a particular purpose

b the duty or obligation for one's actions, decisions, etc.

c the means or materials available to help you achieve a goal

d clearly different or separate

e adapt something to a particular need

f the variety or differences found within a particular group, community, etc.

g people who have graduated from a particular school

h oversee and direct the work or performance of others

B **A** で学んだ語句を使い、以下の英文を完成させましょう。

1. Our school library provides a wide range of .... for research and study.

2. The school supports .... through cultural exchange programs and events.

3. The lifeguards closely .... the swimmers in the pool to ensure everyone's safety.

4. Students have a .... to submit their assignments on time.

5. The company offers .... training in customer service to all its employees.

6. Many .... of our university have gone on to achieve success in various professions.

7. The unique design of the building features .... shapes and lines.

8. The personal trainer will .... the workout routine to meet your fitness goals.

30

Brainstorming

次の問題に取り組み、英語で発信するための準備をしましょう。

A 高校と大学の学びの違いについて、 HINTS を参考にして考えてみましょう。以下に挙げた以外にも思いつくだけ挙げましょう。

☐ *specialized learning*   ☐ *social environment*   ☐

☐   ☐   ☐

HINTS

- How does the level of academic responsibility differ between high school and university?
- Can high school students choose their own daily schedules like university students?

B A で考えたことをふまえて、（   ）内の指示にしたがって、高校と大学の学びの違いを3つの英語の文で書いてみましょう。

1. （unlike を使って）

....

....

....

2. （in contrast を使って）

....

....

....

3. （while を使って）

....

....

....

物事を比較する

物事を比較する場合、比較するための基準が必要となります。比較・対照を表すエッセイやプレゼンテーションでは、対象となる物事を複数の側面から比較評価することがよくあります。その際、何と何がどのような基準や観点で比較されているかを明確にするように心がけましょう。

Useful Expressions

評価や比較の範囲・基準・観点を示す表現

- **As far as** education **is concerned**, critical thinking is more important than memorization.
- **When it comes to** pets, I prefer dogs to cats.
- **In terms of** performance, this computer is faster than that one.
- **From an** environmental **point of view**, prioritizing sustainability is more important than economic growth.
- **As for** my favorite cuisine, I like Italian food best.

比較対象を明示する表現

- **Compared to** last year, the company's profits have doubled.
- John is more knowledgeable **than** his younger brother.

比較を強める表現

- The new car is **much** more fuel-efficient than the previous model.
- His first movie was highly praised, but his second movie was **even** more successful.

Now You Try

次の英文を読み、下の設問に答えましょう。

Living in a residence hall on campus and living off campus are two main options for college students, each with its own advantages. In terms of (❶), living on campus is usually the better option because it provides easy access to classes, the library and other campus resources. In addition, on-campus housing tends to provide more opportunities for students to (❷). ❸With regard to personal space and privacy, however, off-campus housing typically offers more than dorm rooms. Moreover, off-campus housing tends to be quieter and less distracting, allowing students to (❹).

1. 空欄❶ に入る最も適切な語を以下から選びましょう。

   a. cost   b. quietness   c. convenience   d. popularity

2. 空欄❷に入る言葉を自由に考えて英文を完成させましょう。

   ....

   ....

3. 下線部❸に最も近い意味の語句を以下から選びましょう。

   a. Unlike   b. When it comes to   c. In spite of   d. For example

4. 空欄❹に入る言葉を自由に考えて英文を完成させましょう。

   ....

   ....

Present Your Ideas

この Unit で学習したことをもとに、高校と大学の学びの違いについてのプレゼンテーション原稿を完成させましょう。

1 High school and university represent two distinct phases of a student's education, each accompanied by a unique set of experiences and challenges.

In contrast, universities

2 Perhaps the biggest difference between high school and university is

3 On the other hand,

4 Another big difference

5 Finally,

Is Honesty Always the Best Policy?

正直であることは人と信頼関係を築く上で重要な要素であり、一般に美徳だと考えられています。ただし、状況によっては真実を言わない方がよいという考え方もあります。この Unit では、常に正直であるべきかどうかについて考え、英語で意見を述べる練習をしましょう。

Get Started

以下の質問に対して英語で答えましょう。

1. How important is honesty in maintaining a relationship? Explain your answer.

2. Do you always give your honest opinion when someone asks for it? Why or why not?

Honesty Is the Best Policy

1 There is a well-known saying that goes, "Honesty is the best policy." It means that it's better to tell the truth than to lie, no matter what the consequences might be. I agree with this for several reasons.

2 Honesty builds trust in our personal and professional connections. It creates an environment where people can rely on us. They can feel confident that our words are genuine and not just empty promises or attempts to deceive or mislead others, or to avoid accountability. Without honesty, trust can easily be broken, leading to hurt feelings, misunderstandings and damaged relationships.

3 Honesty also advances our personal development. Being truthful to ourselves when we make a mistake means we're taking responsibility for it. We can use the mistake as a learning opportunity. And while there are times when it may be challenging to be honest, particularly when we need to admit a serious mistake or share bad news, truthfulness ultimately results in stronger relationships and a greater sense of self-worth.

4 Dishonesty, on the other hand, can become a complicated pattern of untruths, resulting in a loss of credibility and respect. Moreover, lying may cause harm to people by unjustly damaging their reputation or prompting them to take actions based on false information.

5 In short, honesty is the basis of any healthy relationship. It creates an environment of trust and openness, resulting in stronger and more meaningful interactions, and it gives one a greater sense of self-respect. For these reasons, I believe that honesty is the best policy.

Notes

deceive 欺く　mislead 惑わせる、誤解させる　accountability 責任

Get It Right

本文の内容に合うように、(　　) の中から適切な語句を選びましょう。

1. Honesty creates an environment in which people can (a. depend on others
   b. make empty promises to others).

2. According to the writer, there may be times when (a. lying is acceptable
   b. being truthful can be difficult).

3. Dishonesty can grow to become a complex network of (a. falsehoods
   b. misunderstandings).

Paragraph Summary

 本文の語句を使い、各パラグラフを要約しましょう。
完成したら、音声を聞いて確認しましょう。

1 The saying, "Honesty is the best policy," suggests that telling the truth is preferable to lying, regardless of the 1........................ .

2 Honesty is necessary for building personal and 2........................ relationships, without which 3........................ can quickly be lost.

3 Although honesty can be challenging in certain situations, it is valuable in that it promotes personal growth and a greater sense of 4........................ .

4 When people lie, they risk losing the trust and 5........................ of others, as well as potentially causing 6........................ to those who believe their lies and act upon them.

5 To sum up, honesty is necessary for healthy relationships. It builds trust and 7........................, and enhances a person's self-worth.

A 以下の語句の定義を下の a ~ h から選んで .... に記入しましょう。

deceive ....

withhold ....

perceive ....

truthful ....

acceptable ....

harmony ....

credibility ....

consequences ....

a a state of agreement, peace and unity

b honest; in accordance with the truth

c refuse to give something (especially, information) to someone

d the results of an action or decision

e the quality of being believable and trustworthy

f trick someone into believing something that is false

g suitable, allowed or tolerated

h understand, interpret or become aware of

B **A** で学んだ語句を使い、以下の英文を完成させましょう。

1. He tried to .... her by pretending to be someone else online.

2. The witness's .... was damaged by his dishonest statements.

3. The government decided to .... certain information from the public.

4. Eating with your hands is .... in some cultures.

5. People do not always .... an event in the same way.

6. The orchestra played in perfect ....

7. She was completely .... when she explained her reasons for leaving the company.

8. What are the potential .... of the decision?

Brainstorming

次の問題に取り組み、英語で発信するための準備をしましょう。

A 正直であることが不利に働く場合について、HINTS を参考にして考えてみましょう。以下に挙げた以外にも思いつくだけ挙げましょう。

☐ lead to conflict ☐ compromise privacy ☐ ....

☐ .... ☐ .... ☐ ....

HINTS

• What are some examples of situations where honesty may cause unnecessary harm?

• What are some examples of situations where withholding information may be justified?

B A で考えたことをふまえて、（　　）内の指示にしたがって、真実を言わない方がよいと考えられる具体的な場面を3つの英語の文で書いてみましょう。

1. (It may be better to keep your thoughts to yourself when ...で始めて)

....

....

....

2. (Telling the truth may cause ...で始めて)

....

....

....

3. (White lies can be justified in situations where ...で始めて　※ white lie 罪のない嘘)

....

....

....

意見をサポートする

意見を表すプレゼンテーションやエッセイでは、自分の意見や主張に対してそれをサポートする根拠や具体例を提示する必要があります。まず自分の意見を簡潔に述べてから、その根拠・理由、さらに具体的事例や詳細を説明すると聞き手にとってわかりやすい構成になります。

Useful Expressions

OPINION（意見）

- {**In my opinion**/**In my view**}, winter is the best season of the year.
- **I believe that** renting a home is better than buying one.
- **I am** strongly **against** animal testing for cosmetic products.

REASON（理由）

- **The main reason is that** winter is perfect for enjoying the beauty of nature.
- **One reason for this is that** renting allows you to move more easily.
- **This is because** animal testing is cruel and unnecessary when alternative methods are available.

EXAMPLE/DETAIL（具体例 / 詳細）

- **In particular**, I love the way everything looks when it's covered in snow.
- {**For example**/**For instance**}, if you get a new job in a different city, you can relocate without worrying about selling your home.
- **In fact**, it is now possible for companies to use computer modeling to test their products.

Now You Try

以下の３つの英文を最も自然な流れになるように並び替えましょう。

A: For example, teachers can use a variety of apps and platforms such as Duolingo or Google Classroom to make learning more interactive and fun.

B: In my opinion, students should be allowed to use their smartphones in the classroom.

C: One reason for this is that smartphones can serve as a helpful tool for increasing student engagement and participation.

上で学んだことを参考にして、以下のパラグラフを自分で考えて完成させましょう。

I believe that students should NOT be allowed to use their smartphones in the classroom.

41

Present Your Ideas

この Unit で学習したことをもとに、正直が常に良いわけではないという意見のプレゼンテーション原稿を完成させましょう。

1 *While I agree in principle that honesty is the best policy,*

....

....

....

Here are a few examples.

2 *In situations where telling the truth*

....

....

....

3 *There are some cases where*

....

....

....

4

....

....

....

5 *In conclusion,*

....

....

....

「ギャップイヤー」とは、高校卒業から大学入学までの時期に学業を離れて様々な体験（長期旅行、ボランティア、留学、インターンシップなど）をするための期間で、イギリスなどの国では制度として広く浸透しています。この Unit では、ギャップイヤーを題材に自分の意見を英語で発信する練習をしましょう。

Get Started
以下の質問に対して英語で答えましょう。

1. Why did you choose to go to university?

2. If you could take a year off from your studies, how would you use your time?

Why Students Should Take a Gap Year

1 A gap year is a period of time, usually taken after completing high school, or before entering university, where students take a break from their studies to explore other interests and experiences. During this time, students may choose to travel, work, do volunteer activities or pursue other personal interests.

5 2 There are several reasons why I think students should consider taking a gap year. First, a gap year provides students with an opportunity to step away from their studies for a while. It can help them set future goals, as well as give them renewed energy and focus when they return to their studies.

3 Second, by taking a gap year, students can gain valuable life experiences and 10 perspectives. This may include traveling to new places, learning about different cultures and volunteering or working in a different environment. These experiences enable students to acquire a deeper understanding of themselves, broaden their view of the world and improve their communication skills.

4 Finally, a gap year is an opportunity for students to acquire new knowledge and skills 15 that will help them in the job market. Moreover, students can demonstrate to future employers that they are energetic, curious, self-motivated and able to successfully meet new and challenging situations.

5 In conclusion, a gap year is a valuable opportunity for students to experience new 20 things, gain fresh insights and improve their employability and job prospects. While it may not be suitable for everyone, for those seeking new challenges and a change of pace, a gap year is certainly worth considering.

Notes

job market 雇用市場

44

Get It Right

本文の内容に合うように、（　　）の中から適切な語句を選びましょう。

1. A gap year is a period of time to (a. prepare for university entrance exams
   b. try and experience new things).

2. Students can (a. receive college credits b. gain new knowledge and skills)
   during a gap year.

3. The writer recommends a gap year for students who (a. want to save money
   b. are looking for new challenges).

Paragraph Summary

本文の語句を使い、各パラグラフを要約しましょう。
完成したら、音声を聞いて確認しましょう。

■ A gap year is a break from academic studies taken by students after high school,
or before university, to 1 .... personal and professional interests.

■ A gap year offers students a chance to recharge, reset their goals and return to
their studies with renewed energy and 2 ....

■ Students gain new experiences and 3 .... through travel, cultural
exposure, etc., leading to self-discovery and improved communication skills.

■ A gap year provides students with valuable skills and 4 .... for the job
market. It shows future 5 .... that they have the necessary qualities to
succeed.

■ In short, a gap year offers students new experiences, self-discovery and
improved employability and job 6 .... It is suitable for those looking for
new challenges and a change of 7 ....

A 以下の語句の定義を下の a ～ h から選んで ⋯⋯ に記入しましょう。

broaden ⋯⋯	a chances or opportunities for success
motivated ⋯⋯	b very important or useful
prospects ⋯⋯	c actively participate or become involved in
engage in ⋯⋯	d concerned with money
	e having a strong drive to achieve a goal
unproductive ⋯⋯	f not achieving much; not very useful
laziness ⋯⋯	g expand the scope or range of something
financial ⋯⋯	h the state of being unwilling to work or use energy
valuable ⋯⋯	

B A で学んだ語句を使い、以下の英文を完成させましょう。

1. I need to avoid ⋯⋯⋯⋯ habits that prevent me from achieving my goals.

2. She is ⋯⋯⋯⋯ to pursue a graduate degree to deepen her knowledge and skills.

3. His ⋯⋯⋯⋯ was the main reason why he did not get promoted.

4. The company has promising ⋯⋯⋯⋯ for success in the long term.

5. Studying abroad can ⋯⋯⋯⋯ your perspective and help you appreciate other cultures.

6. The ⋯⋯⋯⋯ report shows that food prices increased 2% from June to July.

7. It's important for students to ⋯⋯⋯⋯ active learning and participate in class discussions.

8. Market research can provide ⋯⋯⋯⋯ information about consumer behavior.

Brainstorming

次の問題に取り組み、英語で発信するための準備をしましょう。

A ギャップイヤーを取得するべきでないという立場について、 HINTS を参考にして考えてみましょう。以下に挙げた以外にも思いつくだけ挙げましょう。

☐ *loss of connections*   ☐ *career delays*   ☐ ....

☐ ....   ☐ ....   ☐ ....

HINTS

- What are the potential financial disadvantages of taking a gap year?
- Can you think of any academic disadvantages of taking a gap year?

B **A** で考えたことをふまえて、（　　）内の指示にしたがって、ギャップイヤーを取得するべきでない理由を 3 つ英語の文で書いてみましょう。

1. （A gap year usually requires ...で始めて）

....

....

....

2. （Taking a gap year ...で始めて）

....

....

....

3. （Students who take a gap year ...で始めて）

....

....

....

誇張や断言を避ける

現在の傾向や将来の予想を表現する場合に、単純に X does ...、X will ...のような表現形式を使うと、事実の誇張や独断的な断言をしているような印象を聞き手に与えてしまうことがあります。誇張や断言を避けるには以下のような表現が役に立ちます。

Useful Expressions

助動詞で可能性を限定する

- Smoking **can** cause lung cancer and other health problems.
- It **may** not be a good idea to rely on other people's opinions when making a decision.

数量詞で数を限定する

- **Many** students struggle to find time to pursue their hobbies.
- **Some** people believe that life exists on other planets.

部分否定を使う

- Being rich does **not always** mean being happy.
- The best college athletes are **not necessarily** successful at the professional level.

副詞（句）で一般的な傾向を述べる

- Traffic accidents are **often** caused by distracted or reckless drivers.
- **In general/Generally**, people enjoy spending time with friends and family.

傾向を表すその他の表現

- Cats **tend to** be more independent than dogs.
- Young people are more **likely to** take risks and try new things than older adults.

Now You Try

次の英文を読み、例を参考にして、下線部❷〜❹を（　　　）の指示にしたがって断定的でない文に書き換えましょう。

In my opinion, ❶working part-time while attending college is not the best option for students. First of all, ❷working part-time negatively affects students' academic performance, as it often prevents them from focusing on their studies. In addition, ❸part-time jobs are demanding and stressful. As a result, ❹students who work part-time experience increased stress levels and reduced overall well-being.

例 下線部❶（部分否定を使って）

working part-time while attending college is not always the best option

for students

1. 下線部❷（助動詞を使って）

....

....

....

2. 下線部❸（副詞を使って）

....

....

....

3. 下線部❹（more likely to を使って）

....

....

....

Present Your Ideas

この Unit で学習したことをもとに、「ギャップイヤーを取得するべきでない」という意見のプレゼンテーション原稿を完成させましょう。

1 Hello everyone. Today I'm going to talk about

2 Firstly,

3 Secondly,

4 Thirdly,

5 In summary,

Is Space Exploration Worth the Cost?

Different Perspectives 3

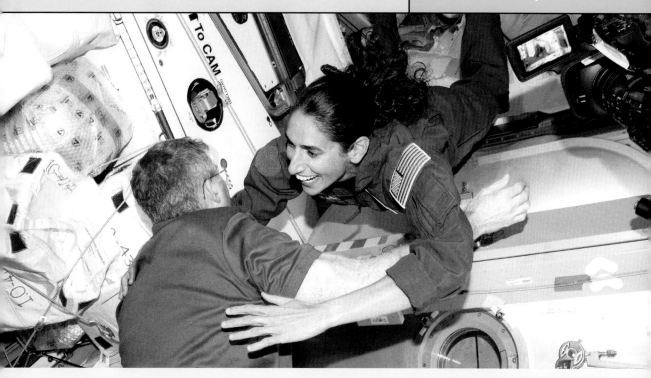

宇宙開発は、宇宙や地球についての理解を深め、人類が持続可能な未来を築くための資源の開発や科学技術の進歩に貢献すると考えられています。その一方で、宇宙開発にはコスト面や安全面などで多くの課題も残されています。この Unit では、宇宙開発を題材に自分の意見を英語で発信する練習をしましょう。

Get Started

以下の質問に対して英語で答えましょう。

1. Does the idea of becoming an astronaut appeal to you? Why or why not?

2. Do you believe that there is intelligent life on other planets? Explain your answer.

The Case Against Space Exploration: Why It Is Not a Wise Use of Money

1 For many people, the idea of space exploration is both fascinating and thrilling. However, in my opinion, it isn't a wise use of money. This viewpoint is supported by a number of important factors.

2 To begin with, the cost of space exploration is extremely high. The funds would be better spent on essential social needs such as healthcare, education, housing and public safety. Some of the money should also be redirected to help fight critical global issues like climate change, poverty, hunger and human rights.

3 Secondly, space exploration can be extremely risky due to the many hazards involved. Astronauts may be exposed to high levels of radiation and suffer from other health issues as a result of living in space for long periods of time. Equipment malfunctions and technical errors could also put their lives in danger. Therefore, it's essential to weigh the risks and benefits before deciding whether to allocate resources to space exploration.

4 Thirdly, the benefits from space exploration are not easily measurable. For instance, the new scientific knowledge and discoveries that come from exploring space may not provide immediate or tangible benefits to society. And while it's important to seek knowledge, it isn't a strong enough reason to spend huge sums of money.

5 Lastly, space exploration is not a priority for most individuals, as it doesn't directly affect their daily lives. The funds should be spent on urgent needs that require immediate attention and have a significant impact on the majority of the population.

Notes

tangible はっきりとした、有形の

52

Get It Right

本文の内容に合うように、（　　）の中から適切な語句を選びましょう。

1. The passage suggests that space exploration (a. may help solve social needs and global issues in the future b. should be given less priority than social needs and global issues).

2. It is suggested that the potential acquisition of new knowledge and discoveries (a. is insufficient reason b. makes a strong case) for allocating funds for space exploration.

3. The writer thinks that space exploration is (a. of equal importance b. of lesser Importance) compared to needs that necessitate prompt action.

Paragraph Summary

 本文の語句を使い、各パラグラフを要約しましょう。
完成したら、音声を聞いて確認しましょう。

1️⃣ Space exploration is fascinating and exciting, but not a 1................................ use of money for a number of important reasons.

2️⃣ Space exploration is very expensive. The funds would be better spent on essential social needs and critical 2...................... issues.

3️⃣ Due to various 3............................, space exploration poses significant risks. The risks and 4...................... must be evaluated before investing resources.

4️⃣ Immediate or 5........................ benefits of space exploration are hard to measure. While seeking 6............................ is important, it doesn't justify the huge cost involved.

5️⃣ Space exploration has no direct effect on people's daily lives. Therefore, the money should be used for pressing needs that impact the 7............................ of people.

A 以下の語句の定義を下の a ～ h から選んで .... に記入しましょう。

allocate	a fill (someone) with motivation or enthusiasm
practical	b the use of something for a particular purpose
potential	c the capability or likelihood of success
invest	d distribute or assign resources
application	e covering a wide variety
extraterrestrial	f put money into something with the expectation of obtaining a profit
inspire	g useful in real-world situations
wide-ranging	h relating to or originating from outside the earth

B **A** で学んだ語句を使い、以下の英文を完成させましょう。

1. The spacecraft detected an unusual signal, suggesting the presence of .... life.

2. The young athlete showed great .... in her first track and field competition.

3. The company offers a .... selection of household products.

4. The city will .... $50 million for the construction of a new high school.

5. The new museum is sure to .... art lovers with its impressive collection of paintings.

6. The .... of technology has changed the way we communicate and access information.

7. Wearing comfortable shoes is a .... choice for a long day of walking.

8. Mary decided to .... her savings in starting her own business.

Brainstorming

次の問題に取り組み、英語で発信するための準備をしましょう。

A 宇宙開発に対する賛成意見について、 HINTS を参考にして考えてみましょう。以下に挙げた以外にも思いつくだけ挙げましょう。

☐ *inspire future generations*   ☐ *promote global cooperation*   ☐ ....

☐ ....   ☐ ....   ☐ ....

HINTS
- What technological advancements have been made as a result of space exploration?
- Can you think of any potential future benefits of space exploration?

B **A** で考えたことをふまえて、（　　）内の指示にしたがって、宇宙開発に対する賛成意見を3つの英語の文で書いてみましょう。

1. (Space exploration can ...で始めて)

....

....

....

2. (Space exploration has the potential ...で始めて)

....

....

....

3. (By exploring space, ...で始めて)

....

....

....

譲歩構文を使う

意見や主張を述べるエッセイやプレゼンテーションでは、「確かに…である。しかし、〜だ」といった「譲歩→反論」という論理展開がよく用いられます。自分と反対の意見や一般論に関して認められるべき点を認めた上で、それとは異なる自分の意見を提示することで、一方的でない説得力のある議論が展開できます。

| Concession（譲歩） | → | Rebuttal（反論） |

Useful Expressions

譲歩構文

- **It's generally believed that** hard work is the key to success, **but** it's important to remember that other factors, such as natural talent and luck, also play a role.
  (譲歩 It's ... success 反論 but ... play a role.)

- **Some people argue that** school uniforms foster a sense of unity among students, **but** I believe they can prevent students from expressing their individuality.
  (譲歩 Some people argue ... students 反論 but ... individuality.)

- **It's true that** online shopping has brought convenience to our lives. **That (being) said**, it has also contributed to the decline of physical stores and local businesses.
  (譲歩 It's true ... lives 反論 That (being) said ... businesses.)

- **Although** social media has made it easier than ever for people to share information, it has also given rise to concerns about the spread of misinformation.
  (譲歩 Although ... share information 反論 it has also ... misinformation.)

Now You Try

以下の例を参考にして、「譲歩→反論」の流れになるように、それぞれの英文を自分で自由に考えて完成させましょう。

例 It's understandable that homework can sometimes be stressful for students, but

it does help them to better understand the course material.

1. Although fast food is delicious and inexpensive, ...

....

....

2. It's true that having a credit card is convenient because it eliminates the need to carry around cash. However, ...

....

....

3. While I admit that living in a big city can be expensive, ...

....

....

4. Some people argue that AI has the potential to increase efficiency and productivity in some industries. At the same time, however, ...

....

....

5. It is often said that technology has made us more disconnected from one another, but ....

....

....

Present Your Ideas

この Unit で学習したことをもとに、宇宙開発に賛成の立場のプレゼンテーション原稿を完成させましょう。

1 *Some people question whether money should be spent on space exploration.*

However,

2 *In the first place,*

To give an example,

3

4

5 *Finally, and perhaps most importantly,*

Leisure Activities & Vacations

忙しい現代人にとって、余暇や休暇は非常に大切な時間です。日々の仕事や学業などの拘束から解放されて心身をリフレッシュすることは、健康で充実した生活を送るために欠かせません。この Unit では、余暇や休暇の過ごし方の種類について考え、英語で分類を適切に表現する方法を学びましょう。

Get Started

以下の質問に対して英語で答えましょう。

1. What kind of leisure activities do you enjoy doing?

2. Where would you like to go on vacation? Explain why.

....

....

....

What's Your Leisure Pleasure?

1 In today's fast-paced and busy world, leisure activities play an important role in our lives, providing a much-needed break from the demands and pressures of our daily routines. These activities can be broadly classified into four main categories: physical activities, intellectual interests, creative hobbies and social interactions. Let's examine each category in more detail.

2 Physical activities promote physical health and well-being. They include sports such as soccer, tennis and basketball, as well as recreational pursuits like swimming, hiking and rock climbing. People who enjoy being physically active are often motivated by a desire for exercise, competition and adventure.

3 Intellectual interests involve activities that stimulate the mind and expand one's knowledge. Reading books, solving puzzles and attending educational workshops and presentations are examples of intellectual leisure activities. People having these types of interests are often driven by curiosity, logical thinking and a keen desire to broaden their understanding of how things work.

4 Creative hobbies enable people to make full use of their imagination and express their artistic talent. Painting, writing, playing a musical instrument and doing handicraft work are popular creative leisure activities. Creative individuals feel a sense of satisfaction through the process of creation and self-expression.

5 Social interactions revolve around activities that promote meaningful connections with others. These activities include attending parties and other social gatherings, volunteering and participating in community events. People who enjoy spending their leisure time interacting with others tend to be outgoing and personable, and derive pleasure from building and maintaining relationships.

Notes

outgoing 社交的な　　personable 人当たりのよい

60

Get It Right

本文の内容に合うように、（　　）の中から適切な語句を選びましょう。

1. Rock climbing falls under the category of (a. physical activities b. creative hobbies).

2. People having intellectual interests are often (a. driven by competition b. motivated by curiosity).

3. Socially active people (a. enjoy the company of others b. derive pleasure from self-expression).

Paragraph Summary

本文の語句を使い、各パラグラフを要約しましょう。
完成したら音声を聞いて確認しましょう。

1 Leisure activities are vital in our busy lives, offering a break from our daily 1........................ . They may be 2........................ into physical, intellectual, creative and social aspects.

2 Engaging in physical activities, including sports and recreational 3........................, improves health while offering opportunities for exercise, competition and adventure.

3 Engaging in intellectual interests activates the 4........................ and promotes the acquisition of knowledge. People in this category are motivated by curiosity and a desire to learn.

4 Creative hobbies let people use their imagination and 5........................ ability. Creative people find fulfillment through creation and 6........................ .

5 Social interactions are about activities that focus on human connections. People who are sociable and friendly, and enjoy forming and continuing 7........................ with others fall into this category.

Vocabulary Builder

次の問題に取り組み、本 Unit に関連する重要語句の意味と使い方をマスターしましょう。

A 以下の語句の定義を下の a ～ h から選んで .... に記入しましょう。

routines ....

relaxation ....

well-being ....

re-energize ....

stimulating ....

recreational ....

immerse ....

leisurely ....

a arousing interest or excitement

b fully involve oneself in something

c the state of being free from tension, anxiety or stress

d regular activities performed habitually

e unhurried; done without haste

f the state of being healthy and happy

g relating to things done for pleasure

h bring energy to someone or something again

B **A** で学んだ語句を使い、以下の英文を完成させましょう。

1. Engaging in hobbies and other interests can enhance one's overall ....

2. This virtual reality game allows players to .... themselves in a lifelike gaming experience.

3. Professor Jones gave a .... presentation about what the world might look like in 100 years.

4. Every morning, Susan takes her dog for a .... walk in the park.

5. After the first term began, students quickly settled into their normal ....

6. Taking a 20-minute nap in the afternoon can .... you for the rest of the day.

7. For many people, a hot bath provides instant .... and stress reduction.

8. The park offers various .... options such as hiking trails and picnic areas.

Brainstorming
次の問題に取り組み、英語で発信するための準備をしましょう。

A 次の表は休暇の過ごし方を4種類に分類したものです。

VACATION TYPE	EXAMPLES
Relaxing vacations	Staying at a luxury resort, spending time at the beach, going for a massage, (❸), etc.
(❶)	Visiting historical landmarks, participating in local festivals, visiting museums, etc.
Adventurous vacations	Rock climbing, mountain climbing, scuba diving, white-water rafting, (❹), etc.
(❷)	Golfing, fishing, cruising, going to theme parks, going to a karaoke bar, etc.

1. ❶と❷に入る最も適切な語句をそれぞれ次から選びましょう。

   a. Recreational vacations   b. Cultural exploration vacations

   ❶.................... ❷....................

2. ❸と❹の例をそれぞれ1つ考えて、以下に記入しましょう。

   ❸.................................... ❹....................................

B 以下の例を参考にして、それぞれの休暇の過ごし方がどのような人に向いているかを英語で書いてみましょう。

例 Relaxing vacations are perfect for *people who simply want to relax and unwind.*

1. Recreational vacations appeal to ....

....

2. Adventurous vacations are ideal for ....

....

3. Cultural exploration vacations are perfect for ....

....

分類する

分類は、物事を共通の特徴にしたがって複数のグループに分けることで情報を整理する働きをします。分類を表すエッセイやプレゼンテーションでは、分類対象となる物事が何種類のカテゴリーに分けられるのかを示した上で、それぞれのカテゴリーについて順番に説明するのが典型的な展開方法です。

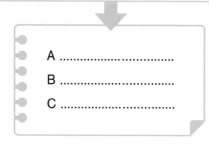

X can be classified into A, B and C.

A ....
B ....
C ....

Useful Expressions

分類の結果を表す表現

• Animals can be {**divided/classified/categorized**} **into** three groups.

分類の基準を表す表現

• Animals can be **classified** into three types {**according to/based on**} their diet.

分類したカテゴリーに言及する表現

• **The first category** is carnivores. They are animals that primarily eat meat.

• **Another type** is called herbivores. Animals that mainly eat plants **fall into this class**.

• **The last group** is omnivores. They eat both plants and meat.

Now You Try

下の表は日本の道路標識を分類したものです。表にしたがって、パラグラフを完成させましょう。

TYPE	DESCRIPTION	EXAMPLES	
Regulatory signs	Indicate prohibitions and restrictions.	Stop signs, speed limit signs, no entry signs, etc.	
Warning signs	Alert drivers to potential hazards.	Slippery road signs, steep hill signs, curve ahead signs, etc.	
Instruction signs	Indicate specific roads or zones, or tell drivers what they are allowed to do.	Parking zone signs, stopping allowed signs, crosswalk signs, etc.	
Guide signs	Provide information about directions, distances, etc.	Direction signs, interchange signs, expressway exit signs, etc.	熱　海 17km Atami

There are more than a hundred different road signs in Japan, but they can be classified into four main types according to their purpose. The first type is

Present Your Ideas

この Unit で学習したことをもとに、休暇の過ごし方を 4 つに分類し、それを伝えるプレゼンテーション
の原稿を完成させましょう

1 *Vacations are a welcome change from day-to-day routines, allowing individuals to*
....

....

They may be categorized into four main types:
....

....*.*

Now I'll explain
....

....

2 ....*vacations offer*..
....

....

3 ....*trips are all about*..
....

....

....

4 ....*holidays are perfect for*..................................
....

....

5 ....*vacations provide opportunities to*.......................
....

....

The Dynamics of Friendships

喜びや悲しみを分かち合ったり、悩んでいる時や困っている時に支えてくれたりする友人は人生において貴重な存在です。この Unit では、友情にはどのような種類があるか、真の友情とはどのようなものかについて考え、英語で分類を適切に表現する方法を学びましょう。

Get Started

以下の質問に対して英語で答えましょう。

1. Would you rather have one or two close friends or many acquaintances? Explain your answer.

2. What are some ways that you and your friends support each other?

....

....

....

Aristotle's Perspective on Friendships

1 The ancient Greek philosopher Aristotle gave great consideration to the nature of friendship and identified three distinct classifications. Each classification helps us comprehend why and how people form relationships and connect with each other. Moreover, by understanding these categories, we can gain insight into the complex
5 nature of friendships.

2 Aristotle's first classification is utility-based friendship. This type of friendship develops when individuals come together to achieve a common goal or mutually beneficial outcome. These friendships typically depend on certain conditions, and often end when the usefulness or advantage ceases to exist.

10 **3** The second classification is pleasure-based friendship. It is characterized by shared experiences and enjoyment. People in these relationships derive pleasure and satisfaction from each other's company and build a strong bond of friendship. Nevertheless, if the pleasure diminishes, or the interests of the individuals change, the friendship may naturally fade away.

15 **4** Aristotle's third and most highly valued classification is virtue-based friendship, which depends on mutual admiration and shared virtues. These friendships are built on trust, respect and a genuine concern for each other's health and happiness. Because virtue-based friendships are rooted in the basic goodness of each individual, they are strong and enduring.

20 **5** In summary, Aristotle's classifications—utility-based friendship, pleasure-based friendship and virtue-based friendship—provide a basic structure to understand the dynamics of friendships. By recognizing and understanding these categories, we can better deal with the complexities and challenges involved in forming relationships with others, and build long-lasting and fulfilling friendships.

Notes

utility 有用性　　diminish 減少する

本文の内容に合うように、(　　) の中から適切な語句を選びましょう。

1. Utility-based friendships (a. often grow to become life-long relationships b. are often short-lived).

2. Friendships that develop as a result of a shared interest are (a. pleasure-based b. virtue-based).

3. Virtue-based friendships are strong and enduring because (a. they are built on a foundation of trust and respect b. the individuals have similar personalities).

Paragraph Summary

 本文の語句を使い、各パラグラフを要約しましょう。
完成したら、音声を聞いて確認しましょう。

1 Aristotle classified friendships into three types. By understanding these classifications, we can obtain 1........................ into the complexities of friendships.

2 A utility-based friendship is formed when individuals unite for a common goal. These friendships depend on specific 2........................ and often end when the benefit diminishes.

3 Pleasure-based friendships are based on shared 3........................ and enjoyment. However, if the pleasure of being together 4........................, these friendships may gradually cease to exist.

4 Aristotle's most highly 5........................ category of friendship is virtue-based. Grounded in natural 6........................, these friendships are strong and long lasting.

5 Aristotle's classifications provide a framework to understand friendship 7......................... Understanding these categories allows us to better face the challenges associated with friendships and build enduring and 8........................ connections.

A　以下の語句の定義を下の a 〜 h から選んで .... に記入しましょう。

bond	....	a	real, true and authentic
mutual	....	b	reliable and deserving of trust
genuine	....	c	a distinctive characteristic
quality	....	d	the state of being kept private or secret
loyalty	....	e	a connection or feeling of attachment between individuals
trustworthy	....	f	a strong feeling of sympathy and concern for the suffering of others
confidentiality	....	g	shared by or common to two or more people or groups
compassion	....	h	faithfulness or allegiance to a person, group or cause

B　**A** で学んだ語句を使い、以下の英文を完成させましょう。

1. A .... doctor is essential for proper medical care and advice.

2. .... towards others helps build a more caring society.

3. The team's success was a result of their .... cooperation.

4. The charming .... of the old bookshop attracts book lovers from all over the city.

5. Despite living in different countries, the two friends maintain a strong ....

6. .... between doctors and patients is essential for building trust.

7. Ted demonstrated .... to his company by being a trusted employee for over 40 years.

8. The teacher's .... interest in her students' education inspired them to work harder.

Brainstorming

次の問題に取り組み、英語で発信するための準備をしましょう。

A 真の友情とはどのような性質によって特徴づけられるかを、 HINTS を参考にして考えてみましょう。以下に挙げた以外にも思いつくだけ挙げましょう。

☐ *loyalty*   ☐ *acceptance*   ☐ ....

☐ ....   ☐ ....   ☐ ....

HINTS

- What qualities do you value most in a friend?
- What kind of friend do you think you can form a lasting bond with?

B **A** で考えたことをふまえて、（ ）内の指示にしたがって、真の友人とはどのような人であるかを3つの英語の文で書いてみましょう。

1. (A true friend is ...で始めて)

....

....

....

2. (A genuine friend is someone who ...で始めて)

....

....

....

3. (A true friend offers ...で始めて)

....

....

....

コロケーションを知る

日本語には「濃いコーヒー」という表現がありますが、英語では ×thick coffee ではなく、strong coffee と言うのが普通です。同様に、×take some sleep よりも get some sleep、×heavily ill よりも seriously ill とするのが自然です。このように、単語と単語には結びつきやすい組み合わせがあり、それをコロケーションといいます。

下の対話の太字箇所はいずれもコロケーションとして使われやすいものです。コロケーションの知識は、自然な英語を書いたり話したりする上で非常に役に立ちます。

Professor: I've been **reviewing your paper**, and I've found a few errors in the data analysis.

Student: Oh no! I'm **terribly sorry**, Professor Brown. I should have **proofread it more carefully**.

Professor: It's okay. **These things happen**, but I would like you to **fix the errors**.

Student: Of course. I'll do it right away. I'll **do my best** to ensure that the paper is up to your standards.

Professor: Thank you. I'm sure you'll **do a great job**.

Useful Expressions

形容詞＋名詞	動詞＋名詞	副詞＋形容詞
a loyal friend	build relationships	deeply compassionate
a faithful companion	offer encouragement	sincerely supportive
a casual acquaintance	show respect	mutually respectful
a caring attitude	develop friendships	genuinely kind
a strong bond	maintain harmony	truly understanding

Now You Try

次のパラグラフを読み、下の設問に答えましょう。

I believe that the qualities that make a good teacher can be divided into three key components. Passion for teaching is one of the most important qualities of a good teacher. A good teacher is passionate about teaching and endlessly patient with their students ❶regardless of their learning pace. Teaching skills are another key component of a good teacher. A good teacher not only ❷(understanding / a / of / has / deep) the subject they teach, but they also have the ability to ❸engage students and help them learn. The third key component of a good teacher is interpersonal skills. A good teacher is able to communicate (❹) with their students, understand their needs and ❺(strong / them / with / build / relationships).

1. 下線部❶に最も意味の近いものを以下から選びましょう。

   a. no matter how quickly or slowly they learn
   b. no matter what subject they study
   c. no matter when they study

2. 下線部❷の語を並び替えて正しい英文を完成させましょう。

   ....

3. 下線部❸に最も意味の近いものを以下から選びましょう。

   a. show respect for students   b. provide support to students
   c. get students involved

4. 空欄❹に入る最も適切な語を以下から選びましょう。

   a. hardly   b. hugely   c. effectively   d. fiercely

5. 下線部❺の語を並び替えて正しい英文を完成させましょう。

   ....

Present Your Ideas

この Unit で学習したことをもとに、真の友情に見られる特徴を 3 つに分類し、それを伝えるプレゼンテーションの原稿を完成させましょう。

1 ....

But what exactly makes a true friend? I believe the qualities that define genuine

friendships can be classified into three general categories:

.... Let me explain what I mean.

2 .... is a fundamental quality of a true friend.

....

....

....

3 .... is another essential mark of a true friend.

....

....

....

4 The third important characteristic ....

....

....

....

5 In short, from my perspective, ...

....

....

....

Stress Among University Students

大学生活にはさまざまな楽しい側面がありますが、時にはストレスを伴うこともあります。試験や課題で忙しい時期や、就職活動の時期などは特にストレスを感じる人が多いでしょう。この Unit では、大学生のストレスの原因と影響について考え、英語で原因と結果を適切に表現する方法を学びましょう。

Get Started   以下の質問に対して英語で答えましょう。

1. What aspects of university life cause you stress?

2. What are some strategies you use to manage stress?

What Stresses Out College Students?

1 Students often go through difficult and stressful times during their university life. Stress may result from a variety of different factors, often affecting students' physical,
5 mental and emotional well-being.

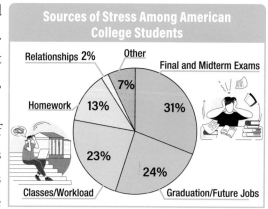

Sources of Stress Among American College Students

Relationships 2%
Other
Final and Midterm Exams
7%
Homework 13%
31%
23%
24%
Classes/Workload
Graduation/Future Jobs

2 The pie graph shows the main causes of stress among American college students. As you can see, almost one-third of students perceive final exams and midterms to be
10 their main cause of stress. This is followed by anxiety about graduation and future employment, at 24%, and classes and workload at 23%. Thirteen percent of students perceive homework to be their main source of stress, while 2% attribute stress to relationships. Seven percent cited other reasons.

3 Stress from exams, classes and workload, and homework all fall under the category
15 of academic pressure, or the pressure to perform well academically. Exams and grades often weigh heavily on the minds of many students, while the large volume of reading and writing assignments and other coursework can be overwhelming.

4 Many students worry about their prospects after graduating and feel uncertain about their career path. This uncertainty can be extremely stressful, as students are faced
20 with making challenging decisions about their future.

5 Finally, social pressure often places significant emotional stress on students, as they strive to make new friends, fit in and maintain healthy relationships. In addition, some students experience homesickness, loneliness or social anxiety, particularly those who are living away from home for the first time.

Notes

weigh heavily on ～に重くのしかかる

Get It Right

本文の内容に合うように、（　　）の中から適切な語句を選びましょう。

1. Tests are the main source of stress for (a. 13% b. 31%) of American college students.

2. Academic pressure includes stress related to tests, classes and workload, and (a. graduation b. homework).

3. Emotional stress may be the result of (a. social pressure b. a heavy workload).

Paragraph Summary

 本文の語句を使い、各パラグラフを要約しましょう。
完成したら、音声を聞いて確認しましょう。

1 University students may experience stress from various 1............................... that affect their physical, mental and emotional health.

2 The 2........................... displays American college students' top stressors, namely: exams, graduation and future jobs, classes and workload, homework and 3......................... .

3 4............................... pressure is a common stressor among students. Exams, 5........................... and a heavy workload can negatively affect their mental health and well-being.

4 As graduation approaches, students often experience stress and anxiety about what they will do next and what their 6........................ holds for them.

5 Social pressure can cause 7....................... stress for students as they struggle to fit in, make friends and maintain relationships. Homesickness, loneliness and social anxiety are also common.

A 以下の語句の定義を下の a ～ h から選んで .... に記入しましょう。

fatigue	a too intense or powerful to be dealt with
chronic	b a heavy load, responsibility, etc. that causes difficulty or strain
overwhelming	c extreme tiredness or exhaustion
distress	d make (someone) annoyed
hectic	e a state of great suffering or discomfort
burden	f have a significant effect on something or someone
irritate	g very busy
impact	h lasting for a long time or happening frequently

B **A** で学んだ語句を使い、以下の英文を完成させましょう。

1. The price increases will .... people's shopping habits.

2. The pressure to meet high expectations can be ....

3. The increased workload placed a heavy .... on employees.

4. Dealing with .... headaches made it difficult for him to do his work.

5. The dog's constant barking began to .... the neighbors.

6. The marathon runner fought through .... and was able to finish the race.

7. She was under a great deal of financial .... after losing her job.

8. After a long and .... week, he looked forward to a relaxing weekend.

Brainstorming

次の問題に取り組み、英語で発信するための準備をしましょう。

A ストレスが大学生にどのような影響を与えるかを、 **HINTS** を参考にして考えてみましょう。以下に挙げた以外にも思いつくだけ挙げましょう。

☐ *sleep problems* .... ☐ *difficulty concentrating* ☐ ....

☐ .... ☐ .... ☐ ....

HINTS

• Have you experienced any changes in your mood during periods of stress?

• Do you turn to any bad habits when you are stressed out?

B **A** で考えたことをふまえて、( ) 内の指示にしたがって、ストレスが大学生にもたらす影響を 3 つの英語の文で書いてみましょう。

1. (Stress can ...で始めて)

....

....

....

2. (Chronic stress may lead to ...で始めて)

....

....

....

3. (When stressed out, ...で始めて)

....

....

....

Say It Clearly

数値の割合を表す

グラフはデータを視覚的に表したもので、プレゼンテーションでよく用いられます。グラフの中で特によく使われるのが円グラフと棒グラフです。円グラフは全体に対する各カテゴリーの割合を、棒グラフはカテゴリー間の大小関係を示すのに適しています。視覚的に提示した情報を英語で適切に表現できるようにしましょう。

Useful Expressions

グラフを導入する表現

- **This pie chart illustrates** the distribution of students at ABC University by nationality.
- **The bar graph shows** the number of books checked out from the library by genre in 2023.

グラフから分かること伝える表現

- **As you can see from the graph**, sales dropped sharply last year.
- **It is clear from the graph that** most voters are in favor of the new law.

割合に関する表現

- {**One in four/A quarter of/Twenty five percent of**} students reported experiencing high levels of stress during exam periods.
- Dairy products {**account for/make up**} 10% of the total food consumed in this country.

概数を表す表現

- {**Nearly/Almost**} two-thirds of students are concerned about their future job prospects.
- In 2020, the population of the city was {**about/approximately**} 6 million.
- The company's profits increased by {**just over/slightly over**} 30% last year.

Now You Try

次のパラグラフを読み、下の設問に答えましょう。

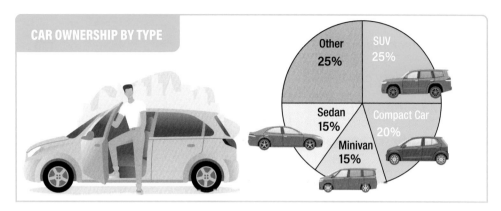

The pie chart shows the percentage distribution of different types of cars owned by a group of 1,000 people we surveyed. As you can see, the most common car type was the SUV (sport utility vehicle), with 25% of the respondents being SUV owners. Next came the compact car, at 20%. Tied for third place were the Minivan and the Sedan, each at 15%. The (❶) 25% reported owning other kinds of cars.

1. パーセントを使わずに SUV の所有者の割合を伝える文を書いてみましょう。

....

....

2. パーセントを使わずにコンパクトカーの所有者の割合を伝える文を書いてみましょう。

....

3. ミニバンとセダンの所有者の割合を伝える文を以下の書き出しに続けて書いてみましょう。

The Minivan and the Sedan each

....

....

4. 空欄❶に入る最も適切な語を以下から選びましょう。

a. remained　　b. remaining　　c. another　　d. rest

Present Your Ideas

この Unit で学習したことをもとに、ストレスが大学生にもたらす影響についてのプレゼンテーション原稿を完成させましょう。

1 Stress can affect university students in a variety of ways. Sleeping and eating patterns are often the first signs of stress. As the graph shows,

Effects of Stress on University Students

Oversleeping	31%
Difficulty sleeping	60%
Decrease in appetite	32%
Increase in unhealthy eating habits	36%

(0 10 20 30 40 50 60 70)

Meanwhile, loss of appetite

2 In addition to the sleep and eating issues described above,

3 Stress can also affect   . For example,

This could result in

4 Finally,

The Baby Bust in Japan

少子化は社会保障制度の維持、経済の活力、自治体の行政機能など、国の社会経済のさまざまな面に影響を与えうる深刻な問題です。この Unit では、日本における少子化の現状について概観し、少子化によって起こる影響、少子化を引き起こしている原因について考えましょう。

Get Started

以下の質問に対して英語で答えましょう。

1. Do you think the declining birth rate in Japan is a concern for the country's future? Why or why not?

2. Why is Japan's population decreasing, while populations in many other countries are increasing?

The Impact of Japan's Low Birth Rate

1 The declining birth rate in Japan has been a topic of much discussion in recent years. Since the 1970s, the birth rate has been on the decline. According to estimates, if the trend continues, the population will decrease from 125 million to 80 million by 2070. This has significant implications for the country's economy, culture and society.

5 **2** One of the most serious consequences of the country's low birth rate is its aging population. As the population ages, the workforce shrinks. This in turn leads to a scarcity of workers. Moreover, the growing elderly population strains the healthcare and social security systems.

3 The low birth rate also significantly impacts the Japanese economy. As fewer young 10 people enter the workforce, the shortage of skilled workers in key industries becomes particularly problematic. It could seriously reduce Japan's economic growth and innovation, as well as its competitiveness in the global marketplace.

4 The housing market is another sector that is significantly impacted by the low birth rate. With couples opting to have fewer children or none at all, the demand for new 15 homes has decreased, leading to a slow-down in house construction and a decline in property values in many areas of the country.

5 Finally, the cultural and social impacts of a low birth rate cannot be ignored. Fewer children could result in a decline in traditional family values, a shift to individualism and materialism, and less participation in community events that have been an integral 20 part of the country's social fabric for generations.

Notes

strain 負担をかける   competitiveness 競争力   social fabric 社会構造、社会の仕組み

Get It Right

本文の内容に合うように、（　　）の中から適切な語句を選びましょう。

1. One result of Japan's low birth rate is (a. a shortage of skilled workers
b. a shrinking elderly population).

2. A decrease in demand for new homes results in (a. higher home prices
b. lower property values).

3. A low birth rate may result in (a. a breakdown of b. a shift towards) traditional
family values.

Paragraph Summary

 本文の語句を使い、各パラグラフを要約しましょう。
完成したら、音声を聞いて確認しましょう。

▉ Japan's low birth rate is expected to reduce the ¹_____ from 125 million
to 80 million by 2070, resulting in major economic, cultural and societal impacts.

▉ One result of Japan's low birth rate is its ²_____ population, causing a
shortage of workers and straining its healthcare and social security systems.

▉ The declining birth rate in Japan will result in a scarcity of skilled workers
in critical sectors, leading to decreased productivity, creativity and global
³_____.

▉ Japan's low birth rate has resulted in a decrease in the ⁴_____ of new
homes and a decline in ⁵_____ values in many parts of the country.

▉ From a cultural and ⁶_____ standpoint, the low birth rate could result
in a decline of traditional family ⁷_____, a shift towards individualism and
materialism, and reduced participation in long-held community events.

A 以下の語句の定義を下の a ~ h から選んで .... に記入しましょう。

prioritize	....	a	the total number of people employed or seeking employment
demographic	....		
retiree	....	b	a person who has permanently stopped working
		c	a regular payment provided to a retired person
maternity	....	d	give greater importance or preference to (something)
workforce	....	e	decrease in size
pension	....	f	the state of being or becoming a mother
		g	relating to the characteristics of human populations
shrink	....	h	a general direction of change
trend	....		

B **A** で学んだ語句を使い、以下の英文を完成させましょう。

1. The company saw a downward .... in sales during the summer months.

2. The .... in the technology industry is rapidly expanding.

3. After a long and active career in business, the .... is enjoying a quiet life.

4. To achieve success, you must .... your goals and stay focused.

5. Washing the wool sweater in hot water caused it to ....

6. The city has experienced major .... changes due to immigration.

7. Mr. Jones has decided to wait until he is 70 before receiving his ....

8. The company offers flexible working hours to support employees during their ....

86

Brainstorming

次の問題に取り組み、英語で発信するための準備をしましょう。

A 日本における少子化の原因について、HINTS を参考にして考えてみましょう。以下に挙げた以外にも思いつくだけ挙げましょう。

☐ *decline in traditional family values* ☐ *job security* ☐ ....

☐ .... ☐ .... ☐ ....

HINTS

- What are the challenges of raising children in Japan?
- What government policies have been implemented to address the low birth rate, and how effective have they been?

B **A** で考えたことをふまえて、(　　) 内の指示にしたがって、日本の少子化の原因を 3 つの英語の文で書いてみましょう。

1. (One reason ...で始めて)

....

....

....

2. (government support という語句を使って)

....

....

....

3. (Many young people ...で始めて)

....

....

....

数値の動向を表す

人口の変動や売上高の推移など、数値の増減や推移をプレゼンテーションやエッセイで報告する場合、数値の変化の特徴に応じた適切な表現を使うことが求められます。以下に紹介する英語表現は、数値の動向を表す際に典型的に用いられるものです。

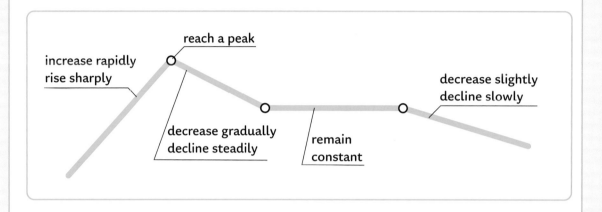

Useful Expressions

数値の動向を表す動詞表現

- Sales of electric cars have been steadily {**increasing/growing/rising**} over the past three years.
- The number of tourists {**decreased/declined/dropped**} sharply in 2020.

数値の動向を表す名詞表現

- There was a dramatic {**increase/growth/rise**} in sales from January to February.
- There has been a slight {**decrease/decline/drop**} in the number of traffic accidents.

数の増減を表す比較表現

- **More and more** people are choosing to live in big cities.
- **Fewer** people are reading books these days.

Now You Try

次の英文を読み、下の設問に答えましょう。

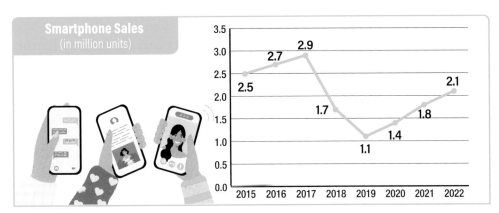

The line graph represents Company A's smartphone sales between 2015 and 2022. As we can see from the graph, ①sales gradually increased from 2015 to 2017, with the number of units sold rising from 2.5 million in 2015 to 2.7 million in 2016 and reaching just under 3 million in 2017.   However, because of Company B's entry into the market, Company A's sales (②) to 1.7 million units in 2018.   In 2019, the number decreased further to 1.1 million.   In order to stay competitive in the market, Company A decided to adjust its pricing model in 2020.   (③) the new pricing strategy, sales started to pick up, climbing from 1.4 million units in 2020 to 1.8 million in 2021 and reaching 2.1 million in 2022.

1. 下線部①を以下の書き出しに続くように書き換えてみましょう。

   there was
   ....

   ....

2. 空欄②に入る言葉を自由に考えて英文を完成させましょう。

   ....

3. 空欄③に入る最も適切な語を以下から選びましょう。

   a. Because   b. Despite   c. Thanks to   d. In addition to

Present Your Ideas

この Unit で学習したことをもとに、日本における少子化の原因についてのプレゼンテーション原稿を完成させましょう。

1 *The cause of Japan's low birth rate can be explained by various factors, but perhaps the main reason behind this trend is*

2 *A second reason behind the low birth rate is*

3 *A third factor is due to*

4 *Finally,*

The Upsides & Downsides of Social Media

ソーシャルメディア（SNS）は、インターネット上で利用者同士が情報共有や交流をするための媒体で、世界中の人に利用されています。この Unit では、ソーシャルメディアによって得られる恩恵とソーシャルメディアの利用による弊害を考察し、英語で是非や賛否を適切に表現する方法を学びましょう。

Get Started

以下の質問に対して英語で答えましょう。

1. How has social media affected the way you communicate with family and friends?

2. What are a few of your favorite social media platforms and why?

....

....

....

Positive Effects of Social Media

1 Social media has undeniably emerged as a crucial aspect of modern-day life. Every day, millions of individuals worldwide spend hours reading Instagram feeds or posting their opinions on various events and issues. And while it may have potential pitfalls, it's important to recognize the upsides that social media offers.

2 For starters, social media platforms offer a convenient way for people to stay in contact with family and friends, regardless of physical distance. Social media has also made it easier for people to connect with others who share similar interests. The resulting online communities offer individuals a sense of belonging, as well as emotional and social support.

3 In addition, social media has made information more accessible than ever before, allowing easy access to a diverse range of news, research and educational sources. This has enormous potential to improve education and promote lifelong learning.

4 Furthermore, social media has become an indispensable platform for businesses to connect and interact with their customers, providing distinct benefits for companies of all sizes. Small businesses can use it to expand their customer base by promoting their products and services to a wider market. Meanwhile, larger companies can utilize it to build brand awareness and customer loyalty.

5 Lastly, social media has allowed minority groups, who may have been ignored or silenced in the past, an opportunity to voice their opinions and concerns. It has enabled individuals to spread awareness about causes they believe in and organize social movements that have the potential to bring about real and meaningful change to society.

Notes

pitfall 落とし穴　for starters まず第一に

92

Get It Right

本文の内容に合うように、（　　）の中から適切な語句を選びましょう。

1. Social media platforms allow people to stay connected despite (a. unreliable internet connections b. being physically separated).

2. Thanks to social media, small businesses can (a. increase their customer base b. reduce business expenses).

3. The passage suggests that social media can help (a. large businesses b. minority groups) realize important societal changes.

Paragraph Summary

 本文の語句を使い、各パラグラフを要約しましょう。
完成したら、音声を聞いて確認しましょう。

1️⃣ Social media has become an essential part of daily life, connecting millions of people 1................... through various platforms.

2️⃣ Social media helps people stay connected with loved ones, share interests and find support through online 2..................... .

3️⃣ Social media provides easy access to various 3..................... of information, which have the potential to enhance education and learning.

4️⃣ Social media is vital for businesses of all 4..................... . Small businesses can attract more customers, while larger companies can boost 5..................... recognition and loyalty.

5️⃣ Social media empowers 6..................... groups to voice their opinions and concerns, raise awareness and promote positive change through social 7..................... .

Vocabulary Builder

次の問題に取り組み、本 Unit に関連する重要語句の意味と
使い方をマスターしましょう。

A 以下の語句の定義を下の a ～ h から選んで .... に記入しましょう。

upside	....	a	an intentional deception of others for personal gain
indispensable	....	b	absolutely necessary or essential
misinformation	....	c	a positive aspect of something
bullying	....	d	the crime of stealing someone's personal information
fraud	....	e	repeatedly harming or harassing someone less powerful
anonymous	....	f	without revealing one's name or identity
identity theft	....	g	deliberately give a false description of (something)
misrepresent	....	h	false or inaccurate information

B   **A** で学んだ語句を使い、以下の英文を完成させましょう。

1. .... is a crime where someone obtains and uses another person's personal information without their permission.

2. One .... of technology is that it makes communication easier.

3. The company's advertisements often .... their products' effectiveness.

4. A large amount of money was given to the charity by an .... donor.

5. The article contained a lot of .... about the health benefits of the energy drink.

6. In today's society, smartphones are considered .... tools.

7. Teachers play an important role in recognizing and putting a stop to ....

8. The man was found guilty of .... for stealing company money for over 10 years.

Brainstorming

次の問題に取り組み、英語で発信するための準備をしましょう。

A ソーシャルメディアを利用するデメリットについて、HINTS を参考にして考えてみましょう。以下に挙げた以外にも思いつくだけ挙げましょう。

☐ *privacy concerns* ☐ *cyberbullying* ☐

☐ ☐ ☐

> **HINTS**
> • What are the negative psychological effects of social media use?
> • What are the potential risks of using social media as a source of information?

B A で考えたことをふまえて、（　）内の指示にしたがって、ソーシャルメディアの短所を3つの英語の文で書いてみましょう。

1. (Social media can ...で始めて)

2. (Another concern ...で始めて)

3. (more likely to experience という語句を使って)

つなぎ言葉を使う

つなぎ言葉（transition expression）とは、論理関係を明示する語句のことで、聞き手または読み手が話の流れをスムーズに理解するのを手助けする標識の役割をします。つなぎ言葉を適切に使用すれば、プレゼンテーションやエッセイを聴衆や読者にとってよりわかりやすいものにすることができます。

下のパッセージの太字箇所はつなぎ言葉としてよく使われるものです。それぞれのつなぎ言葉がどのような働きをしているかを考えてみましょう。

> There are both advantages and disadvantages to homework. **On the one hand**, it allows students to review what they have learned in class. **Moreover**, it also helps them develop important skills such as time management and discipline. **On the other hand**, excessive homework can lead to negative consequences for students. **For example**, students may experience stress and fatigue when overloaded with homework assignments. **As a result**, the quality of their work may decline, which could lead to a decrease in motivation and academic performance. **All in all**, homework can be helpful for students, but it should be assigned sensibly; **that is**, it's important to assign an appropriate amount of homework to help students learn, but not so much that they are overwhelmed by it.

Useful Expressions

対比・対照	in contrast, however, on the {one/other} hand など
追加	in addition, moreover, furthermore, besides など
言い換え	in other words, namely, that is (to say) など
例示	for example, for instance, as an illustration など
因果関係	as a result, for this reason, consequently など
まとめ・結論	to {conclude/summarize}, in {conclusion/summary}, all in all など

Now You Try

次の英文を読み、下の設問に答えましょう。

With the rise of e-commerce, online shopping has become the norm for many consumers, but we should keep in mind that it has both pros and cons. On the positive side, (❶). Moreover, online stores often have a wider selection of products available than physical stores. (❷), there are some disadvantages to online shopping. For example, (❸). In addition, there is always the risk of identity theft and fraud when you shop online. In conclusion, online shopping has a number of advantages, but it is important to (❹).

1. 空欄❶に入る言葉を自由に考えて英文を完成させましょう。

   ....

   ....

2. 空欄❷に入る最も適切な語を以下から選びましょう。

   a. However   b. Consequently   c. All in all   d. In other words

3. 空欄❸に入る言葉を自由に考えて英文を完成させましょう。

   ....

   ....

4. 空欄❹に入る言葉を自由に考えて英文を完成させましょう。

   ....

   ....

Present Your Ideas

この Unit で学習したことをもとに、ソーシャルメディアの短所についてのプレゼンテーション原稿を完成させましょう。

1 *While social media has revolutionized the way people interact and communicate,*

it has also brought forward a number of significant issues, one of which is

....

....

....

2 .... *is another major concern with social media.*

....

....

....

....

3 *A third significant issue associated with social media is*

....

....

....

....

4 *Finally,*

....

....

....

....

Homestay or Stay Home?

ホストファミリーとの共同生活の中で異文化を直接体験できるホームステイは、留学中の滞在方法として特に人気があります。この Unit では、ホームステイを利用するメリットとデメリットについて考え、英語で是非や賛否を適切に表現する方法を学びましょう。

Get Started

以下の質問に対して英語で答えましょう。

1. If you could do a homestay anywhere in the world, where would it be and why?

2. Do you think a homestay abroad is suitable for you? Why or why not?

....

....

....

Homestays May Not Be for Everyone

1 Homestays abroad are popular among Japanese students because of the various benefits they offer. However, it's important to carefully consider several factors before deciding whether or not to participate in one. Let's take a closer look at some of those considerations.

5 **2** One of the biggest challenges encountered by many students during homestays is the language barrier. Communication difficulties arise when they struggle to understand the language spoken by their host family. Moreover, students may feel frustrated when host family members speak too quickly or use unfamiliar vocabulary and expressions. As a result, some students may avoid interacting with one or more host relatives.

10 **3** A second potential problem is culture shock. Adjusting to the customs, values and way of life of the host family can be challenging for some students. This is particularly true among those who have never traveled abroad before, as they may be unfamiliar with the cultural differences and find it hard to adapt to new customs and behaviors.

4 Additionally, homesickness can pose a significant challenge for Japanese students, 15 particularly when they are away for an extended period. The longing for familiar surroundings, the company of family and friends and the sense of comfort from their home country can negatively affect their overall mood and well-being.

5 Lastly, homestay students often experience limited independence. Host parents may have strict rules and 20 expectations that students must follow, which can restrict their freedom to make personal decisions regarding their daily 25 schedules and leisure activities.

Get It Right

本文の内容に合うように、（　　）の中から適切な語句を選びましょう。

1. Some homestay students may avoid communicating with host relatives who
   (a. are much older than them   b. speak well above their level of understanding).

2. Culture shock can be particularly challenging for students with (a. no prior
   international travel experience   b. experience living in a number of different
   countries).

3. Strict family rules may cause students to (a. neglect their academic
   responsibilities   b. wish for more independence).

Paragraph Summary

 本文の語句を使い、各パラグラフを要約しましょう。
完成したら、音声を聞いて確認しましょう。

1 Although homestays abroad offer various benefits to Japanese students, there

are several 1........................ that should be considered before deciding to take part

in one.

2 A major challenge during homestays is the language 2........................, which

could cause communication difficulties and potential frustration for students.

3 Another possible problem is culture 3........................, as students may find it

4........................ to adjust to the new customs, values and way of life of their host

families.

4 Extended periods away from home can result in 5........................ for Japanese

students, impacting their 6........................ and overall well-being.

5 Homestay students may have little 7........................ due to host family rules and

expectations, thereby restricting their personal decision-making.

次の問題に取り組み、本 Unit に関連する重要語句の意味と使い方をマスターしましょう。

A 以下の語句の定義を下の a ～ h から選んで .... に記入しましょう。

struggle	....	a	real or genuine
adapt	....	b	not causing any trouble or difficulty
long for	....	c	have a strong desire for (something)
hospitality	....	d	face challenges or difficulties in achieving something
		e	directly experienced or observed
authentic	....	f	change in order to fit in with new circumstances
enriching	....	g	the act of providing a friendly and comfortable environment for guests
hassle-free	....	h	adding value or positive experiences to something
first-hand	....		

B **A** で学んだ語句を使い、以下の英文を完成させましょう。

1. The hotel staff is known for its excellent service and ....

2. The online reservation process was quick and ....

3. Many students .... with public speaking due to nervousness.

4. His internship gave him .... experience in event planning.

5. After examining the painting, experts determined that it was ....

6. New employees often need to .... to the company's culture.

7. Watching the children playing in the park made him .... his carefree childhood.

8. The museum's interactive displays provide an .... learning opportunity for visitors.

102

Brainstorming

次の問題に取り組み、英語で発信するための準備をしましょう。

A ホームステイの長所について、 HINTS を参考にして考えてみましょう。以下に挙げた以外にも思いつくだけ挙げましょう。

☐ *convenience*   ☐ *security*   ☐

☐   ☐   ☐

HINTS

• What does a homestay experience offer that classroom learning does not?

• How can participating in a homestay contribute to personal growth?

B **A** で考えたことをふまえて、（　）内の指示にしたがって、ホームステイの長所を3つの英語の文で書いてみましょう。

1. (Students can...で始めて)

2. (Homestays abroad provide ...で始めて)

3. (Living with a local family ...で始めて)

動名詞主語を使う

原因・理由・手段・条件などの意味は、副詞節や副詞句以外にも、＜動名詞主語＋使役の意味を持つ動詞＞という形で表現される場合もあります。以下に紹介するのは典型的なパターンです。形式と意味をセットでおさえておきましょう。

Useful Expressions

S は O が〜するのに役立つ（SVO ＋ 原形不定詞 / to 不定詞）

- **Exercising regularly** helps you (to) lead a healthy lifestyle.

S によって O が〜する（SVO ＋ 原形不定詞）

- **Listening to this music** makes me feel energized.

S によって O が〜する（SVO ＋ to 不定詞）

- **Rejecting the proposal** might cause all investors to withdraw their support.
- **Banning plastic bags** will force consumers and retailers to go green.

S のおかげで O が〜できる（SVO ＋ to 不定詞）

- **Learning English** has enabled me to access a wealth of information.
- **Studying with peers** allows you to exchange ideas and gain different viewpoints.

S が原因で O が〜できない（SVO ＋ from 動名詞）

- **Getting enough sleep** will prevent you from feeling tired during the day.
- **Being bullied** didn't stop her from pursuing her dreams.

Now You Try

次の英文を読み、下の設問に答えましょう。

An increasing number of Japanese companies are adopting English as their official corporate language, but there are both advantages and disadvantages to this practice. One advantage is that it helps (❶). In addition, ❷(promote / a common / having / language / can) unity among employees. However, there are some potential drawbacks as well. For example, ❸(English / use / the / requiring / of) in the workplace may create a situation where competent employees with limited English proficiency are prevented from contributing their insights, while those fluent in English are more likely to make their voices heard regardless of their job performance. In addition, ❹if workers are forced to communicate in a language they are not proficient in, they may experience feelings of frustration, exclusion and reduced job satisfaction.

1. 空欄❶に入る言葉を自由に考えて英文を完成させましょう。

2. 下線部❷の語を並び替えて正しい英文を完成させましょう。

3. 下線部❸の語を並び替えて正しい英文を完成させましょう。

4. 下線部❹を forcing と cause という語を使って書き換えてみましょう。

Present Your Ideas

この Unit で学習したことをもとに、ホームステイの長所についてのプレゼンテーション原稿を完成させましょう。

1 A homestay abroad represents a valuable opportunity for Japanese students to

....

....

....

....

2 An overseas homestay enables students to

....

....

....

....

3 Another advantage

....

....

....

....

4 A final consideration that favors participation

....

....

....

....

AI: A Double-Edged Sword

AI（人工知能）は、学習や推論などの人間の知的活動をコンピュータによって人工的に実現するもので、製造、医療、教育、金融などの幅広い分野で応用されてきています。この Unit では、AI 利用の長所と短所について考え、英語で是非や賛否を適切に表現する方法を学びましょう。

Get Started

以下の質問に対して英語で答えましょう。

1. What comes to mind when you hear the term "artificial intelligence"?

2. What do you think the relationship between AI and humans will be in the next 10 years?

Checking Off the Plus Points of AI

1 Artificial Intelligence (AI) has the potential to transform both individuals' lives and society as a whole in numerous positive and impactful ways. Through careful examination, we can uncover some of the key benefits that AI has to offer.

2 Better Efficiency: AI has the capacity to take over monotonous and time-consuming
5 tasks that are typically handled by humans, such as data entry, quality control and customer support. This increases productivity, reduces costs and frees up workers so that they can focus on more complex tasks that require human skills.

3 Personalization: AI can analyze customer data and offer personalized recommendations, thereby improving customer satisfaction and loyalty. For instance,
10 by examining a customer's purchase history, AI can suggest products they may be interested in. This personalized approach enhances the customer experience, building a stronger relationship between businesses and their customers.

4 Enhanced Decision-Making: AI can analyze large amounts of data much faster and more accurately than humans. This is especially useful in finance, where AI can
15 identify patterns and predict future trends based on historical data. For example, AI can analyze stock market data to forecast price movements and assist with investment decisions. By utilizing AI's data processing abilities, companies and individuals can make more informed decisions and attain better financial results.

5 Improved Safety: AI can significantly enhance safety in
20 many ways. It can enable self-driving cars to avoid collisions, monitor and predict equipment failures, improve cybersecurity, and detect and prevent accidents from happening in factories and on construction sites.

Notes

uncover 明らかにする monotonous 単調な collision 衝突

Get It Right

本文の内容に合うように、（　　）の中から適切な語句を選びましょう。

1. AI can recommend products a customer might like by (a. introducing the most popular ones   b. reviewing the customer's past purchases).

2. AI's ability to quickly analyze large volumes of data is especially beneficial in the (a. financial sector   b. fine arts field).

3. Improved cybersecurity is used as an example of AI's (a. enhanced safety capabilities   b. superior efficiency).

Paragraph Summary

 本文の語句を使い、各パラグラフを要約しましょう。
完成したら、音声を聞いて確認しましょう。

---

1 AI has the power to bring significant and positive transformations to people's lives and the broader 1......................... .

2 AI promotes better 2........................... by automating various tasks, allowing workers to concentrate on responsibilities that only 3....................... can perform.

3 AI can examine data and deliver recommendations based on individual preferences and interests, thereby improving the business-customer 4........................ .

4 AI's data analysis capabilities enable faster and more accurate predictions of economic 5..........................., helping companies and individuals make smarter 6...................... decisions.

5 AI can greatly improve 7........................ by preventing collisions in self-driving cars, predicting equipment breakdown, improving cybersecurity and stopping workplace 8....................... from happening.

A 以下の語句の定義を下の a ～ h から選んで .... に記入しましょう。

transform ....

threaten ....

biased ....

displacement ....

ethical ....

unintended ....

discrimination ....

vulnerable ....

a not objective or fair; influenced by prejudices

b easily harmed or attacked

c change (something) in form, character, etc.

d the act of taking the place or position of something or someone

e unfair or prejudicial treatment of individuals or groups

f not planned or meant

g be likely to harm or cause damage

h relating to principles of what is right and wrong

B **A** で学んだ語句を使い、以下の英文を完成させましょう。

1. We should all work together to create a world that is free from ....

2. Humor can sometimes lead to .... misunderstandings or confusion.

3. If the forest fire is not brought under control, it could .... nearby towns.

4. Elderly individual are more .... to certain health risks.

5. The renovation project aims to .... the old warehouse into an apartment building.

6. The new mall has led to the .... of many small shops in the area.

7. To gain customers' trust, it is important for businesses to operate in an .... manner.

8. Tom's evaluation of the product was considered .... because of his personal connection to the company.

Brainstorming

次の問題に取り組み、英語で発信するための準備をしましょう。

A AI を利用する上での短所について、HINTS を参考にして考えてみましょう。以下に挙げた以外にも思いつくだけ挙げましょう。

☐ *security risks* .... ☐ *reduced creativity* .... ☐ ....

☐ .... ☐ .... ☐ ....

> **HINTS**
> • What potential effects might the widespread use of AI have on the job market?
> • What othical concerns might the use of AI in decision making raise?

B A で考えたことをふまえて、（　）内の指示にしたがって、AI を利用する上での短所を 3 つの英語の文で書いてみましょう。

1. （AI could lead to ...で始めて）

....
....
....

2. （As AI systems become more advanced, ...で始めて）

....
....
....

3. （Relying too much on AI ...で始めて）

....
....
....

将来の予測や可能性を表す

テクノロジーの進化、気候変動の影響、経済状況の見通しなど、将来に関しての推測や展望は、確定的な事柄としてではなく予測として伝えるのが普通です。将来の予測や可能性を表す表現には以下のようなものがあります。

Useful Expressions

予測・推測を表す表現

- The upcoming jazz concert **is {expected/predicted} to** attract more than 5,000 attendees.
- **It is {expected/predicted} that** the typhoon will make landfall tomorrow morning.

数値の予測を表す表現

- The cost of healthcare **is {estimated/projected} to** increase significantly over the next decade.
- **It is {estimated/projected} that** the population of this city will decrease by 2% next year.

可能性・潜在性を表す表現

- The completion of the renovation project **is likely to** be delayed by a few weeks.
- **It is {possible/likely} that** 3D printing technology will make our lives more convenient.
- Failure to preserve the environment **{can/may/might}** lead to a serious shortage of essential natural resources.
- **There is a {possibility/chance} that** we will find life on other planets.
- The breakthrough in medical research **has the potential to** save countless lives.

Now You Try

次の例を参考に、( ) 内の語句を用いて以下の各文を将来の予測や可能性を表す文に書き換えてみましょう。

例 3D printing replaces traditional construction methods. (the potential)

3D printing has the potential to replace traditional construction methods.

1. The world population will reach 9.7 billion by 2050. (It is estimated)

2. Extreme weather events occur more frequently due to climate change. (predicted to)

3. Space tourism becomes accessible to the general public. (likely to)

4. The global sea level will rise one meter by 2050. (possible)

5. Self-driving vehicles will become the norm in many parts of the world. (a possibility)

Present Your Ideas

この Unit で学習したことをもとに、AI を利用する上での短所についてのプレゼンテーション原稿を完成させましょう。

1 *The rapid advancement of AI has brought exciting innovations and benefits for individuals, businesses and society. However,*

. Let's explore a few of these threats.

2 :

3 :

4 :

The Rural Depopulation Challenge

日本では少子高齢化とともに大都市への過度な人口集中が続いており、過疎化の進む地方部では労働力の不足や公共サービスの低下などの問題が深刻化しています。この Unit では、地方過疎化の問題について考え、問題解決に関して英語で適切に発信する方法を学びましょう。

Get Started

以下の質問に対して英語で答えましょう。

1. What are some advantages of living in the country?

2. What are some disadvantages of rural life?

Implications of Rural Depopulation

1 Rural depopulation is a term used to describe the decreasing number of people living in rural areas. In recent years, the social, economic and environmental implications of rural depopulation have become highly problematic in Japan.

2 One of the most urgent problems associated with rural depopulation is the aging of
5 the population. As more and more younger people are moving to larger urban centers, rural communities are gradually becoming older, with a growing proportion of elderly residents. With the passing of elderly residents, family farms and other businesses face uncertain futures, and unoccupied houses, many of which are in serious disrepair, can be seen throughout the country.

10 3 Another issue arising from rural depopulation is the increased burden on essential services like healthcare and education. With fewer residents, the cost of providing and maintaining these services increases. This can lead to service reductions or even complete closures, significantly reducing the quality of life for those who remain.

4 Declining economic activity is another challenge linked to rural depopulation. For
15 local businesses, a smaller population in the community means a smaller customer base, lower profits and the possible risk of eventual closure. Business closures result in unemployment, further contributing to the (　　　　　　) downturn in economic activity.

5 Lastly, when rural areas experience a decline
20 in population, the natural environments and life forms often suffer. This occurs when empty farmlands and other natural spaces are invaded by non-native species, causing a decline in the native plants and animals.

Notes

depopulation 人口減少, 過疎化　passing 死

116

Get It Right

本文の内容に合うように、（　　）の中から適切な語句を選びましょう。

1. Many rural houses are empty because (a. their elderly owners are gradually passing away   b. elderly home owners are moving in with their children).

2. Fewer residents in rural communities means (a. higher costs for basic services   b. lower utility bills for everyone).

3. Rural depopulation results in (a. an economic downturn   b. a larger customer base for local businesses).

Paragraph Summary

本文の語句を使い、各パラグラフを要約しましょう。
完成したら、音声を聞いて確認しましょう。

1 The declining number of residents in 1................................ areas of Japan has led to significant social, economic and environmental challenges.

2 The 2................................ population in rural areas is faced with challenges as younger residents relocate to cities. The future of businesses becomes unpredictable and houses become vacant with the 3................................ of older residents.

3 Rural depopulation strains essential 4................................ such as healthcare and education, leading to increased costs, service cutbacks and reduced quality of life.

4 Rural depopulation leads to reduced 5................................ activity due to fewer customers, lower profits and subsequent business closures. Closures lead to 6................................ and a further decline in business operations.

5 Rural depopulation can lead to the loss of plants and animals that are native to the area, as abandoned areas may be 7................................ by non-native species.

次の問題に取り組み、本 Unit に関連する重要語句の意味と使い方をマスターしましょう。

A 以下の語句の定義を下の a ~ h から選んで .... に記入しましょう。

incentive ....

infrastructure ....

urbanization ....

conservation ....

underserved ....

migrate ....

abandon ....

implement ....

a the process of people moving from rural areas to cities

b put (something) into action

c not having adequate access to necessary resources or services

d something that motivates someone to do something

e the protection and preservation of natural resources

f move from one place to another (for better living conditions, etc.)

g leave or give up something completely and finally

h the basic systems and services that support society

B **A** で学んだ語句を使い、以下の英文を完成させましょう。

1. Due to heavy rain, they decided to .... their plan to climb the mountain.

2. We need to place more importance on energy .... in our daily lives.

3. The workers were motivated by the .... of a large bonus for completing the project on time.

4. Access to technology can help people living in .... communities.

5. The university will .... a new curriculum next year.

6. One of the challenges of .... is a shortage of affordable housing.

7. The city is investing a large amount of money in improving its aging ....

8. People often .... to cities in search of better employment opportunities.

118

Brainstorming

次の問題に取り組み、英語で発信するための準備をしましょう。

A 地方過疎化を解決する方法について、 HINTS を参考にして考えてみましょう。以下に挙げた以外にも思いつくだけ挙げましょう。

☐ *promote telework*　　☐ *support the agriculture sector*　　☐ ....

☐ ....　　☐ ....　　☐ ....

HINTS
- How can we encourage young people to stay in rural communities?
- What measures can be taken to Improve rural infrastructure?

B **A** で考えたことをふまえて、（　　）内の指示にしたがって、地方過疎化の解決策を 3 つの英語の文で書いてみましょう。

1. （One possible approach ...で始めて）

....

....

....

2. （To encourage young people to stay in rural areas ...で始めて）

....

....

....

3. （To make rural living more attractive ...で始めて）

....

....

....

問題・解決策を論じる

問題解決型のエッセイやプレゼンテーションは、問題とその解決策を論じるものです。最初に対処すべき問題の現状や将来的な影響を説明し、続いてその問題を解決するための具体的な方法や手段を説明するのが一般的な展開パターンです。以下に紹介する表現を参考にしてみましょう。

Useful Expressions

問題を表す表現

- **One of the world's biggest {issues/challenges/problems}** today is our heavy reliance on *fossil fuels.

  *fossil fuels 化石燃料

影響を表す表現

- This over-reliance can **have serious {consequences/implications} for** the environment.

- It can {**lead to/result in/contribute to**} various problems such as air pollution and *greenhouse gas emissions.

  *greenhouse gas 温室効果ガス

目的を表す表現

- (**In order**) **to** tackle this issue, we must implement stricter emissions regulations.

- We need to shift to renewable energy sources **so that** we can reduce our *carbon footprint.

  *carbon footprint カーボン・フットプリント（商品やサービスの原材料調達から廃棄・リサイクルまでの間に排出される温室効果ガスの CO$_2$ 換算量）

手段・方法を表す表現

- **By** switching to alternative energy sources, we can *pave the way for a cleaner, greener future.

  *pave the way for ～への道を開く

Now You Try

次のパラグラフを読み、下の設問に答えましょう。

Obesity is a serious problem in the United States today, with about ①(as / of / classified / adults / 40%) obese. Because this condition is often linked to serious health problems such as diabetes and heart disease, it (②) to rising healthcare costs and places a significant burden on both individuals and the healthcare system. One way to combat the obesity problem is to incentivize food companies to offer healthier products at reasonable prices. This will help consumers (③). Early education on healthy eating habits can also be effective. Teaching children about balanced diets early on may (④).

Notes obesity 肥満   diabetes 糖尿病   combat ～と戦う

1. 下線部①の語を並び替えて正しい英文を完成させましょう。

2. 空欄②に入る最も適切な語を以下から選びましょう。

   a. increases   b. results   c. causes   d. contributes

3. 空欄③に入る言葉を自由に考えて英文を完成させましょう。

4. 空欄④に入る言葉を自由に考えて英文を完成させましょう。

Present Your Ideas

この Unit で学習したことをもとに、地方過疎化の解決策についてのプレゼンテーション原稿を完成させましょう。

1 *Rural depopulation has become a major problem in Japan, requiring effective solutions to minimize its negative impacts on rural communities. Today I'd like to suggest four potential solutions for the following related problems:*

..., ..., and ....

2 ....

....

....

....

3 ....

....

....

....

4 ....

....

....

....

5 ....

....

....

Plastic Waste Issues & Actions

プラスチックごみによる海洋汚染は、生態系の崩壊や健康被害などにつながる重大な問題です。この問題を解決するためには私たち一人一人がプラスチックごみの削減に取り組む必要があります。この Unit では、プラスチックごみ問題について考え、問題解決に関して英語で適切に発信する方法を学びましょう。

Get Started

以下の質問に対して英語で答えましょう。

1. What are some plastic items that you use regularly?

2. How has your perspective on plastic waste changed over the past few years?

Plastic Overload

  Plastic waste, including such items as bags, bottles and packaging, poses a serious threat to the environment and ecosystems. Unlike organic materials
5 like paper and wood, plastics don't break down quickly and can remain in

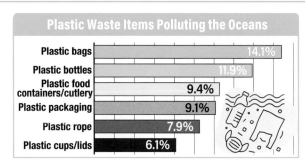

the environment for hundreds of years. Consequently, plastic can accumulate in natural environments and cause significant harm.

 Plastic waste in oceans is another major concern. Of the top ten ocean pollutants,
10 six are plastic. The graph above shows these items. Plastic bags top the list, accounting for about 14% of ocean waste, while plastic cups and lids round out the list at around 6%. Together, these six items account for almost 60% of ocean waste. When plastic waste accumulates in the ocean, marine animals can get caught in plastic bags and rope or mistake them for food, leading to significant harm, including injury or death.
15 Microplastics, which are small plastic particles, can also be consumed by marine life, causing a range of negative effects on their health and well-being.

 In addition, the process of manufacturing, transporting and disposing of plastic is a major source of greenhouse gas emissions such as carbon dioxide and methane. This contributes to climate change and other environmental problems.
20 Lastly, the economic consequences of plastic waste should not be overlooked. The cleanup of plastic pollution is very costly, and its presence can adversely impact the tourism industry. Tourists may choose to avoid beaches and other natural environments that are littered with plastic garbage, leading to potential economic losses in the tourism sector.

Notes

break down 分解する

Get It Right	本文の内容に合うように、( ) の中から適切な語句を選びましょう。

1. Plastics are (a. organic b. inorganic) materials, so they don't break down easily.

2. The passage states that (a. six of the top ten ocean pollutants are plastic
   b. about 60% of plastic waste ends up in oceans).

3. According to the passage, plastic waste may (a. discourage tourists from visiting
   natural areas b. encourage tourists to be more environmentally responsible).

Paragraph Summary		本文の語句を使い、各パラグラフを要約しましょう。 完成したら、音声を聞いて確認しましょう。

① Because plastic is inorganic and therefore does not 1................................ down
quickly, plastic waste can cause severe environmental problems.

② Plastic waste in oceans is a major concern, with six plastic items among the top
2................................. Accumulated plastic waste harms marine animals. The animals
may get caught in bags or rope, or 3................................ them, as well as microplastics,
for food.

③ Plastic production, transportation and disposal generates 4................................
gases, contributing to 5................................ change and other environmental issues.

④ The economic impact of plastic waste is significant, with substantial costs
associated with cleanup efforts and negative effects on the 6................................ industry.

A 以下の語句の定義を下の a 〜 h から選んで .... に記入しましょう。

minimize ....

alternative ....

debris ....

ecosystem ....

accumulate ....

pollutant ....

marine ....

dispose of ....

a a substance that makes air, water or soil dirty or poisonous

b relating to the sea or ocean

c a choice different from the usual or conventional one

d a network of living organisms and their interactions with the environment

e make (something) as small as possible

f get rid of something properly

g gradually gather or increase over time

h scattered fragments of broken or discarded objects

B **A** で学んだ語句を使い、以下の英文を完成させましょう。

1. Exercising regularly and eating a healthy diet can help .... health risks.

2. Rising sea levels are a threat to coastal communities and .... life.

3. Maintaining a healthy .... requires careful management.

4. Over time, unused items can .... in storage spaces.

5. In case of rain, we have planned for an .... indoor activity.

6. This brochure explains how to .... various unburnable items.

7. The chemical .... killed most of the fish in the lake.

8. After the storm, the beach was covered with ...., including bottles, cans and broken branches.

Brainstorming

次の問題に取り組み、英語で発信するための準備をしましょう。

A プラスチックごみ問題を解決するために個々人ができることについて、HINTS を参考にして考えてみましょう。以下に挙げた以外にも思いつくだけ挙げましょう。

☐ *avoid single-use plastics*　☐ *participate in clean-up events*　☐ ....

☐ ....　☐ ....　☐ ....

> **HINTS**
> • What are some small changes that individuals can make to reduce plastic waste?
> • How can individuals help spread awareness about plastic pollution?

B A で考えたことをふまえて、（　）内の指示にしたがって、プラスチックごみ問題を解決するために私たちができることを3つの英語の文で書いてみましょう。

1. (When we go shopping, ...で始めて)

....

....

....

2. (When ordering a drink for takeout, ...で始めて)

....

....

....

3. (We can also ...で始めて)

....

....

....

熟語表現を使う

隣接しない2つの語句が組になって使われる表現を相関語句、複数の語句が結び合わさって1つの前置詞と同等の働きをするものを群前置詞といいます。これらはいずれも熟語として覚えておくとよいでしょう。代表的な相関語句と群前置詞には以下のようなものがあります。

Useful Expressions

代表的な相関語句

- **Both** my sister **and** I are studying abroad this semester.
- This shopping bag is **not only** functional **but also** environmentally friendly.
- You can attend the workshop **either** online **or** in person.
- The weather is **neither** too hot **nor** too cold during this season.
- He was **so** tired after the meeting **that** he fell asleep immediately.
- This book covers a wide variety of topics, **from** history **to** science.
- The city's population increased significantly **between** 2015 **and** 2020.

代表的な群前置詞

- **According to** the weather forecast, there's a chance of rain tomorrow.
- He decided to walk to work **instead of** commuting by car.
- **In terms of** fuel efficiency, this car is superior to all others.
- **Regardless of** whether the team wins or loses, I admire their hard work.
- **In spite of** being injured, he participated in the marathon.
- The outdoor concert was canceled **due to** bad weather.
- We've seen a significant increase in sales **thanks to** the new marketing strategy.

Now You Try

次のパラグラフを読み、下の設問に答えましょう。

Food loss is a serious problem that occurs at all stages of the food supply chain, (❶) production to distribution to consumption. ❷A United Nations report says that about one-third of all food produced is lost or wasted each year.

In order to effectively reduce food loss, the combined efforts of governments, businesses and individual consumers are essential. At the government level, investing in the development of innovative preservation technologies is a possible step towards reducing food loss. For businesses, using data analysis to accurately forecast demand can ❸(prevent / and / both / help / overproduction) spoilage. At the individual level, each consumer can contribute to reducing food loss by buying only what they need and storing leftovers properly instead of (❹).

1. 空欄❶に入る最も適切な語を以下から選びましょう。

   a. between   b. from   c. either   d. both

2. 下線部❷を according to という語句を使って書き換えてみましょう。

   ....

   ....

3. 下線部❸の語を並び替えて正しい英文を完成させましょう。

   ....

   ....

4. 空欄❹に入る言葉を自由に考えて英文を完成させましょう。

   ....

   ....

Present Your Ideas

この Unit で学習したことをもとに、プラスチックごみ問題の解決策についてのプレゼンテーション原稿を完成させましょう。

1 Plastic waste has become a major environmental issue that governments and industry need to seriously address. However, there are also many steps that individuals can take to

....

....

2 The pyramid chart below shows

.... As you can see, Recycle is at the bottom

of the pyramid, followed by ....

.... and finally, ... at the top of the chart.

Let's examine these ways in terms of what individuals can do to solve the problem.

3 Recycle: Separate plastic waste and avoid mixing it with non-plastic items.

Repurpose: ....

Reuse: ....

Reduce ....

Refuse: ....

Ways to Manage Plastic Waste

Refuse
Reduce
Reuse
Repurpose
Recycle

4 In addition to these five methods, individuals can ....

.... ,

.... and ....

....

クラス用音声CD有り（別売）

Presentable
—Writing Clear Opinions
論理的な英語プレゼン原稿の書き方

2024年2月20日　初版発行

著　者　Robert Hickling / 八島 純

発行者　松村 達生

発行所　センゲージ ラーニング株式会社

　　　　〒102-0073　東京都千代田区九段北1-11-11　第2フナトビル5階
　　　　電話 03-3511-4392
　　　　FAX 03-3511-4391
　　　　e-mail: eltjapan@cengage.com
　　　　copyright © 2024 センゲージ ラーニング株式会社

装丁・組版　　藤原志麻（クリエイド・ラーニング株式会社）

編集協力　　　クリエイド・ラーニング株式会社

本文イラスト　秋葉 あきこ

印刷・製本　　株式会社 ムレコミュニケーションズ

ISBN 978-4-86312-425-7